Utah or Bust

Tommy Kirchhoff and writers from Wild Utah

Enjoy this
and come back
to Utah!
7/5/02

Cover Illustration by
Kevin Duffy

Published by
Transcending Mundane Inc.

For information, additional copies, or
Tommy Kirchhoff's first book,
"Nuts in the Woodwork," address
Transcending Mundane, Inc.
PO Box 1241
Park City, UT 84060
free@wildutah.net

ISBN 0-9666422-1-X

Table of Contents

1. Tommy Kirchhoff.........................1

2. Sky.........................73

3. Dustin Sturges.........................84

4. Mike Reberg.........................101

5. Andrew Haley.........................109

6. Jim Moran.........................118

7. Mark Driver.........................129

8. Al Fonzarelli.........................141

9. Andy Baillargeon.........................148

10. Rock Oakeson.........................155

11. Babbage.........................161

12. Contributors.........................164

Foreword by Clare Goldsberry

2002 Unofficial Utah Winter Olympics Language Guide

A handbook of Mormon-speak for foreigners coming from outside the State of Utah

The following terms are things you absolutely MUST know if you expect to survive your stay in Utah. This handbook is essential to helping you understand various Mormonisms, interpreting Mormon language euphemisms, and keeping you from looking too out of place.

LDS: This acronym could have many meanings, and it is usually asked in a sentence like this: "Are you LDS?" Not to be confused with "Have you done LSD?" My husband was prescribed medication for his high blood pressure once that caused him to get LDS (Limp Dick Syndrome), a condition his doctor had never heard referred to as LDS. My husband then had to explain the difference between BEING LDS and GETTING LDS. You can BE LDS and GET LDS, but I think it's against church teachings to GET LDS, because if you GET LDS it is difficult to BE-GET children, and everyone knows that it is a rule that to BE LDS you have to have lots of children.

If anyone asks, "Are you LDS?" just smile, and say, "Only when I see fat women in black spandex." (Leave it up to them to interpret that one)

If you are a woman and someone asks you, "Are you LDS,? just smile and say, "Only when I'm with Dr. Timothy Leary."

Ward Meeting House: This is a common architectural structure in Utah. In other parts of the world you might call these buildings "churches," but in Utah, they are Ward Meeting Houses. They can be easily recognized by the slender, phallic symbol atop the spires of each one; these are so you won't confuse Christian Churches (whose spires have crosses) with the Mormon version of a "church." The phallic symbol has special meaning in Utah, since polygamy was and still is (among the fundamentalist faction of the sect) a very big thing (so to speak).

Ward: a specific geographic area comprised of about 150 or so families. Chicago also has wards, but only the political kind run by the local Mafia. Mormon wards are run by the Mormon version of the Mafia called the Bishopric. (Yes, you heard right. We're back to that phallic symbol thing again) I had a Bishop one time who was a prick, but I digress from our lesson.

Stake House: Be careful if someone asks you if you'd like to go to the "stake" house. Make sure it is spelled "s-t-e-a-k" as opposed to "s-t-a-k-e." Unlike a steak house where you can get charbroiled, medium rare tenderloins and T-bones, the Stake House is a place where you can be roasted by the Stake President if you haven't been minding your P's & Q's as a good Mormon should. The Ward Bishopric answers to the Stake President, who can sometimes be a bigger prick than the Bishop-ric!

Garments: No, this doesn't refer to all the outerwear skiers must don before hitting the slopes. These are "Temple Garments," sometimes referred to as "funny underwear." It is also sometimes called "magic underwear" because good Mormons who have been through the Temple get special protection by wearing this underwear, which is similar to long-johns with short sleeves and legs that go just to the knees. You may notice the outline of these "garments" under the shirts or blouses of many people in the area, which marks them as VGM (Very Good Mormons), as they've been able to get past the interrogation of the Bishopric, and the grilling at the Stake House by the Stake President, and obtain a Temple Recommend (see next term) to go through the Temple and win the privilege of wearing these "Garments."

Temple Recommend: As noted above, you need to pass two interrogations to obtain a permit to get into the Mormon Temple. It's a bit like obtaining a driver's license in that you have to prove you are worthy of the privilege before getting your permit. Obeying all the rules of Mormondom is key to getting a Temple Recommend. No smoking, no drinking, no coffee or tea, and you must be attending church regularly and paying a full tithe (see next term) to be allowed a Recommend.

This Recommend is only good for one year, unlike your driver's license, which is good for 10 or 20 years. The state trusts you to remain a good driver for longer than the Mormon Church trusts you to be a good Mormon.

Tithe: Unlike most church organizations that depend on donations, Mormons require a full tithe, which means a full 10 percent of your GROSS income. Can you believe? Even the IRS cuts you some slack and requires you only pay taxes on your NET income. No wonder the Mormon Church is the wealthiest religious corporation in the known world. You have all these people like ex-quarterback Steve Young, hotelier J. Willard Marriott's family, and baseball hero Orel Hershiser paying huge chunks of their GROSS income to the church. That's GROSS, all right!

Temple Square: This is a famous Utah landmark. It is a section in downtown Salt Lake City that is the site of the Mormon Temple, built by the pioneers in the late 1800s. It's noticeable because of the gold statue of the "Angel Moroni" on one of the spires. If you go to Temple Square, beware of young men and women in suits, smiling way too much for people who've been conscripted to tell you a strange story of angels bringing gold plates from heaven and dead Apostles appearing to deliver "truth" that only people on LSD (not to be confused with LDS) could make up.

You can tour the visitor's center, but don't ask to go through the Temple. They'll tell you that you need a Temple Recommend to do that, and if you refer back to that term, you'll know it's really something you want to take a "pass" on. Besides, if you or any of your relatives are Masons, you pretty much get the drift of what goes on in the Temple.

The "Y": This refers to BYU or Brigham Young University, in Provo, just south of Salt Lake City—not The "Y" as in YMCA, known for giving swimming lessons to its members. In Mormon-dom, The "Y" is an important place. It's where young men go for an education, and where young women go to hunt for an educated, prospective husband. So, don't go looking for The "Y" in order to do a few laps in the pool, because most likely all you'll find at The "Y" in Utah is a bunch of young women looking for husbands.

Word of Wisdom: You will not see Mormons drinking tea, coffee or alcohol, or smoking tobacco, which might strike you as odd. This is due to a Mormon rule known as the "Word of Wisdom." Obedience to this rule is critical to one's standing in the Mormon Church, and part of the test one must pass to get a Temple Recommend. Although they avoid coffee and tea, Mormons are known to get their caffeine fix in other ways, such as the guzzling of Coca-Cola, Mountain Dew, Jolt or other caffeine-laden sodas that the church doesn't forbid. Chocolate is also okay. Alcohol has been a bone of contention in Utah for decades. Olympic attendees are lucky that Utah changed its liquor laws to accommodate winning the Games, or else you'd be stuck with having to cart cases of your favorite drink into restaurants, then be forced to drink the entire stash before leaving. The whole thing has to do with Mormons not wanting other people to enjoy life and have fun. After all, if they can't have fun, why should anyone else? But, Mormons' reward is their ticket into the Temple, where they can receive all the secret passwords to get into heaven. It doesn't get much more fun than that!!

So, when you come to Utah this winter to enjoy the Winter Olympics, print out a handy copy of this guide and keep it in your pocket for quick reference in the likely event that a nicely dressed, smiling young man or woman will approach you and ask, "Are you LDS?"

Tommy Kirchhoff

Gentleman Start your Modars

From "radar," the homosexual universe came up with a great word: gaydar. Gaydar is the rare ability to sniff out a gay person through voice, gestures or whatever means of recognition it might take to do so. (Jack on Will & Grace is the master of gaydar)

This word is just one in an entire lexicon that represents an ability to recognize something specific. Someone with laydar would have the gift of recognizing whether someone else wants to sleep with him or her. Haydar (or jaydar) is the capacity to detect marijuana. Liedar is knowing when someone is feeding you a line of BS.

Here in Utah, there is a specific system of dichotomizing residents. I call it Modar. Because of the radical nature of Mormonism (undeniably radical), people living in Utah must figure out whether or not the person they meet is a Mormon—and it works both ways.

Mormons invented modar. From the beginning, they needed to know if the new guy was someone they could trust, or someone they could try to convert. Even Brigham Young took the attitude, "Are you in, or are you out?"

These days, modar is getting more sophisticated, and evidently, easier to use. It's probably slipped by you a thousand times, but one of the first questions a Mormon will ask is, "Are you from Utah?" Notice the question is not a polite, "Where are you from?" "Are you from Utah?" is first level modar. It means, "Are you a Mormon?" Most transplants let that one go by all day long. "I'm from Connecticut," sizes up about 80 percent of everybody. But if you answer "yes," one of the next questions is likely to be, "What ward are you from?"

Clever non-Mormons have come up with a question that's just as sneaky. "Are you a coffee drinker?" Coffee's hip, happening, and most people drink it—except true Mormons. Coffee consumption is, by the way, a secondary modar.

You see, one clue is not enough. The eventual question by either a Mormon or a non-Mormon is "Are you LDS?" One has to work up to this through many clues, because he or she must absolutely know the answer to the question before it is asked. I love the bumper sticker "RULDS2"—total modar.

A CTR ring is a primary indicator of a Mormon. It stands for "Choose the Right." I've seen that as a bumper sticker too, and it means, "I'm LDS—no messin' around."

If someone swears like a trucker, talks about sex or drugs, drinks alcohol, or smokes cigarettes, you can pretty much assume he or she is not Mormon. There are, however, some Mormons that will drink a beer on Pioneer day, then get on your case for the tiniest joke you make about the LDS Church. (If the church has one downfall, it's that Mormons have no sense of humor when it comes to their wacky lifestyle—undeniably wacky)

When a Mormon swears, you'll know it. "Oh my heck" is

2

clearly Mormon (and honestly, it offends me very deeply). "Fetch!" is merely a Mormon synonym for f*ck. "Gol" seems to be a minor cuss—and "scrud"... I have no idea.

And speaking of language, the accent and dialect set of a native Utahan is fairly particular. It's formally known as Utahnics. It's marked by clipped "t" sounds, and a short beat between syllables. The word "teacher" would be pronounced "teat - chur." Again, the accent alone could belong to a native, non-Mormon, but if you hear, "Sister Jent-sen is my new spear-tchual living teat-chur," mark it as a strike.

First names are another part of language that point in the direction of Mormonism. Male names are many times feminized, and female names are many times made masculine. Most of the time, they're just strange. So if you meet a guy named Amen, Bryce or DeeWayne, or a chick named Maygene, Nathana or Ottalyn, mark that also as a strike.

I've heard some pretty far out stuff that Mormons do for methods of modar. I heard they will put a hand on your back to feel for garments (Mormon underwear—if you didn't know). I've heard they will ask strange questions in a group like, "Are we among friends?" Or how about if your new dentist asks you, "Your teeth are so clean—what ward do you belong to?"

My only advice is to be aware. Modar should be used only for good. It is a means of understanding, asking questions and trying to get along. In the end, segregation is always a losing game.

100 Dirty Words (2)

The reluctant son of a Mafia don
chose smartly to draw the curtain;
for while in his house, high heels and a blouse,
the smell of gay pride was for certain.
He spent winter days sans cute negligees,
at a two-run converging "SLOW" sign.
In ski patrol red, he worked—but his head
dreamed daisies and shopped Calvin Klein.

Now this little lad had a powerful dad
whose sight was as straight as his chin.
And if he had seen that his son was a queen
he'd prob'ly have poofter done in.
But the son had a guise for inquisitive eyes
that held him in ranks of all men.
With a right-clever mind, his linguistics refined,
he impressed with the might of his pen.

His elegant words were always preferred
for their exaltation to snow.
They prompted a grin and read masculine
in a way that no one would know.
His gay friends all laughed at his dark holograph
and pushed him to scream, "I'm a fruit!"

But our hero just yearned for this bane to be burned,
and powerfully penned like a mute.

He pondered a way to show he was gay
without a keen cut to his throat.
But much his chagrin, pulled the curtain again;
in black fishnet stockings he wrote:
"I want to be where I can grow out my hair
and gaze atop great snowy buttes.
On steeps my fear molts by the clutch of my Strolz
as I push down through tight, rugged chutes."

When this poem was done, wasn't missed by a one
and drew cheers on three tones of shtick.
The mob called it "Tough!"
"Behave!" cried the cream puffs;
and patrollers said, "Dude, that was sick."
Though he tickled the fags with metaphorical shags,
gave patrol and the family some pride,
this imprisoned nance didn't victory dance.
In fact, he just wanted to hide.

He toughed out the season for vertical reason,
but his thoughts of out-coming grew dim.
Then April he gained a Pulitzer reign
and his tyrannical father approached him.
He said to his son as he pulled out his gun,

"I can't say I'm into this powder.
But I'm not just a thug, come give Dad a hug;
oh my heck, I couldn't be prouder."

In a life-threatening choice, son hardened his voice
said, "Dad this may come a surprise.
I once touched a girl and I started to hurl—
don't kill me, but I only like guys."
Dad drew a deep breath that exhaled like death;
raised his hand as he started to speak.
"I swear on this pinky, I too was a twinky,
and I still like to drag twice a week."

6

Honey, don't forget the billy club—we're flying Southwest

Southwest is the single most stressful airline one can choose. What makes it so uncomfortable? The boarding process.

With any other airline, one sits comfortably reading a book, or talking on the cell phone—satisfied that his or her seat can be had by no one else. On Southwest, a time is announced when passengers may stand in line to receive a boarding pass. Every person with a ticket is guaranteed a seat. But not one of them will just let it happen.

You see, there's some human psychological stymie that compels jockeying for position. Because no seat is reserved for anyone, every passenger regresses back to childhood. They all want to be first in line, they all want shotgun. So they get in line. The counter attendant must repeat to every person in line that it's not yet time to be in line, and to please have a seat. After getting burned by the attendant, people start to "hang around." This creates a high-stress zone around the counter.

The counter attendant begins to heat up. After every third or fourth person in line approaches, she announces over the PA that it is not yet time to stand in line, and to please, please have a seat.

People still want to be first. Their gazes toggle intensely between the counter attendant and the clock. They begin to experience the same level of stress experienced by the CEO of a failing fortune 500 company. People sit on the floor adjacent the counter. Others sit on the edge of their seats—one foot cocked back, ready for push off. Everyone keeps a maximum distance of 15 feet between themselves and the counter. They all know the jockeying will soon begin, and they certainly don't want to miss anything.

After the mind-numbing litany of discouragement, both vocal and amplified, the counter attendant again wonders why she works for Southwest. The vortex of compression pulses around the counter. Some passengers will drift too close; Southwest chick has no problem banging these fools a second time.

Then the moment comes. There wasn't supposed to be a line, but one materializes instantly. Even passengers who weren't paying attention for that fleeting moment knee-jerk out of their seats and into position.

The line is four people wide and place-marked with elbows. It's turgid and throbbing; but this pre-flight phase is a kindergarten cakewalk compared to what will come.

The frumpy, plastic boarding passes are issued in turn. Passengers placate like a jungle cat over a fresh kill. The intensity of the moment soothes briefly—that is until the mayhem of pre-boarding.

Minutes before, the blaze rekindles. Southwest passengers

rush the gate area, frothing at the mouth. It's a wonder they don't hand out billy clubs for boarding passes. The Southwest Airlines counter attendant calmly announces that "any passengers with small children, or those needing extra assistance may now board." This is the point that the riot starts. 70-year-old men will knock you down to board with the 3-year-olds. Women with walkers have the right-of-way; but they'll assert this vigorously. They'll rack forward like a chugging bulldozer, knocking both you and the 70-year-old rugby player out of the way.

By now, the counter attendant has ducked down in a corner, tied a band around her bicep, and is madly tapping at an artery. Mothers with infants are smashing their way to the front. Mormons are bribing the gate attendants. The pilots are gulping Jack Daniels like some oceanic 7-11 drink. The murderous intensity of this moment leaves the $60 you saved on your ticket a short-term memory fizzle.

Once you're on the plane, it's pretty much business as usual. The stress is over, and you can certainly find a seat. If you take a look around, you will undoubtedly find that you are a member of some bizarre, character circus. The people who fly Southwest are exceptionally, shall we say, eclectic.

The thing I'm still shaking my head at is the job of the counter attendant. How do they find people for this job? Do they tell them in the interview, "This job is a little stressful, but you can drink or smoke pot before you come in..."

Who knows? But I don't recommend Southwest if you're pregnant, have a heart condition, or you're under 48 inches tall.

Hung Up On Numbers In Utah

It's not psychotic to say that all things quantified will soon be adjusted. You want the test? Just pick a number. Your age, a TV channel, any accounting entry. No matter what the figure looks like now, if you factor in a little time it will certainly change.

For that matter, let's just start with time. Can somebody explain this hysteria with setting a watch ahead 15 minutes? I mean, are these ergomaniacs really fooling themselves into thinking they're early? Or do they obsess on the notion that they're on time because they were able to plan "15 minutes out?"

Daylight Savings Time is nothing more than a neurosis created by people afraid of the dark. Set it ahead, roll it back. Lather, rinse, repeat. A lifetime of resetting your watch. The only thing DST has going for it is consistency in it's change—except for places like Indiana that don't observe DST, or places like Arizona that use two clocks. With DST the time can be set semi-annually no matter how many days in a calendar year or who the lunatic is leading the charge.

Thanks to Julius Caesar, the calendar year 46 BC had 445 days. Caesar figured out that every fourth year had been needing an extra day (LeapDay); so he considered how many days the calendar was off by, stretched the year out 80 days to clean things up, and decreed that LeapYears would have an added day to adjust for the irregularity, (back then, March 1st was the first day of the year). Then, a little over 1600 years after Caesar became the human pincushion, Pope Gregory XIII chopped out 10 days and absolved that years ending in "00" would not have this LeapDay. It wasn't until the 19th century that astronomers' calculations revealed the under-compensation of Greggy; they then feathered in another exception—that years ending in "00" divisible by 400 would have the Leap Day. Great! Are we getting close yet? Not really, because we started tracking time with computers; now we can't even tell for sure if a programming glitch like Y2K will be the end of the world. And hey! Let's do it again in 2038!

Here in Utah, the number 2000 was just a slight anxiety before the nervous breakdown. 2002 is the number we're all manic about. And as we all commonly create dementia about 1 number or another, let's review the digits that really reflect our insanity in Utah. In Utah, if your 15th wife is 16, its 10 years and 10 thousand dollars.

If you're 21 you can 3.2 'till 1:00 a.m.; but it takes 2 times as much to achieve .08. What that really boils down to is you just pee 2wice as much. Of course the Utah DABC wouldn't understand because none of those zeros will have one drink.

"Friday" is just a fancy word for the sixth day of the week. There is very little work-difference between it and the seventh day of the week. It's almost state law that nothing happens on the first day of the week.

If your heading west into Salt Lake, you can drive 70 on 80, but only until you hit State Street (which is zero). Someone tell me it's not crazy that 2100 South runs East-West and 300 West runs North-South. So if you're looking for the intersection of those two streets, you can either go to 296 West 2100 South, or 2075 North 300 West. Now that's arithmomania!

If you're trying to get the four-one-one on the Park City nice-price, here's the norm: pay 56 K prices for 28 K service; a quarter in the fiscal third can cost 50, but it might last longer than a half. If you live in the 84060 ZIP code, your area code is 435. Heber City is also 435, and a tiny 12 miles away—but it's long distance.

In some other places, the "deviants" can bet $1000 on lucky # 7—but not here. Here you can secretly bet your friend that the post office is still open at five; but when he doubles down to see you send something out, make sure you're inside the door. The #1 auto repair place will take 4 days to fix 1 switch—then they'll charge you double. If your skis are over 190 cm, you could be construed as "1986." The numerical difference between "resigning" and getting canned is the sum of rumors divided by the set of people telling them.

And still, these matrices are all changing, but some we can subtract. Like this: a Weber basin acre/foot of replacement water is about $136 per year. That buys you 325,850 gallons. A typical golf course is said to use 18 million gallons of water per season, or approximately the same volume required as a town of 9,000 residents. (And guess what—typical golf courses do not exist in the 2nd driest state). So as the number of proposed golf courses changes and goes up, what will happen to the price of water? Hmmm. A crazy person might say, "Conserve water—the golf courses are thirsty."

11

Utah Porn Awards

Governor Might Luvit enters, stage left

(extended applause)

Luvit: "Thank you (smiles, blushes). I'm pleased to be hosting this year's Ohyadewme Awards for outstanding efforts in pornography. Utah is a terrific place to conceal the overzealous viewing and production of pornography, and this year's awards mark a new high. To get the juices flowing, we have a short clip for you from the upcoming film *The Emperor's Blue Tube*."

(fiery porn clip is projected on big screen; audience begins to wiggle in their seats; clip ends; applause)

Luvit: "Turgid... I had an on-the-way-over-here joke ready to go, but now I need to get off...stage. So without further ado, please welcome S.L.U.T. president Mitts Onme to present the award for best independent film with a budget under five thousand dollars."

(applause; Luvit exits stage right; Mitts Onme enters stage left)

Onme: "Thank you Might. I'm a handsome man, thank you. Presenting the award for the best independent film with a budget under five thousand dollars. The nominees are: *The Legend of Bulging Pants*, Provo Productions (clip plays); *Blast Away*, Fling&Swing Films (clip plays); and *Thirteen Lays* by ZionTribe (clip plays). (Onme opens envelope) And the Ohyadewme goes to... *The Legend of Bulging Pants*, Provo Productions.

(applause; Provo Productions representative Tim Pullrekmend offers a mindless thanks; accepts the brass phallus; Onme and Pullrekmend exit stage right; Luvit enters stage left)

Luvit: "Now that's an award the whole family can enjoy. And speaking of enjoyment, there's nothing more fun than trying to decimate Utah's natural environment with irresponsible industry. So to present this year's award for best independent film with a budget over five thousand dollars, please welcome Utah's corrupted congressmen Chimp Handsome and Piss Cannon."

(applause, Luvit exits, Chimp and Piss enter)

Chimp: "So like, porn is cool, huh!" (applause erupts; Cannon snickers uncontrollably)
Cannon: (shaking nervously) "He, he, I wank myself...a

lot." (audience goes silent)

Chimp: "Sure Piss, we all flip the little fiddler. So like, anyway, porn is a 58 billion dollar industry, and it's still on the rise, he he. High-speed internet has enabled so many perverts to access (looks left; producer is gritting his teeth) um, cool stuff... but anyway—the nominees for this years award for best independent film with a budget over five thousand dollars are: *All The Pretty wHores*, The Lykes of Dykes & Strypes (clip plays); *Wonder Toys* by Missionary's Position (clip plays); and *Glad-he-ate-her*, Tri-Anything Pictures (clip plays)... Tasty grubbin'... And the Ohyadewme goes to... *Glad-he-ate-her*, Tri-Anything Pictures."

(applause; Tri-Anything Pictures' Yank Williams accepts the brass phallus and yammers out a snoozer; if it weren't for an incendiary porn clip on the big screen, the audience would be gone)

Might Luvit: "All right, now this place is really rockin'! This industry's all about doin' it. I do it; you do it, we film it and everybody watches it—then they all do it! Some do it fast and some do it slow, but nobody gets it done like Sinator Borin' Snatch. So to present this year's award for the porn film with almost some sort of plot, please welcome Sinator Snatch."

(enters, exits, bla, bla, bla)

Snatch: "Yes, hello. Anyone here seen Traffic? I thought it blew, and I didn't even get off—a ha ha, haha haha—oh. Right then. This year's award for plot is somewhat of a mystery to me. I'm not into plot. I just get it done. Anyway, the nominees for plot are: *Gay It Forward*, Boy Scouts Rn't Us (clip plays); *Almost Laid Us*, Runaway Niece Motion Pictures (clip plays); and *How the Grinch Poled Chris Moss*, produced by DreamJerks (clip). And the Ohyadewme goes to...(has trouble opening envelope)... *Gay It Forward*, Boy Scouts Rn't Us."

(applause, god the crappy speeches—aren't porn movies bad enough?)

Luvit: "Local works are the staple of Utah's porn industry. Let's remember back to the first day MerryYacht Hotels offered pay-per-spew porn movies. *Debbie Does Draper*, and Bring'em Young's *Old Enough To Go The Store* are nostalgic looks at a time when porn was young and fresh. MerryYacht's scorching new *Mormon Miracle Orgy* was actually filmed in This Is The Place park. MerryYacht will hold exclusive screenings of their newest films, *Gooin' Up My Garments* and *Scandel's Only Skin Deep* in Heber next week. Only Utah's worthiest will be invited. Speaking of scandal, here to present the award for the genre 'Britney Spears internet porn,' please

13

welcome our hometown Molympic scandalists, BigTime Belch and Heave Johnson."

(you know the score)

Heave: "We're innocent."
Belch: "Ya, we didn't do nothin'. We'll present this award, but we didn't do nothin' that y'all didn't want us to do; so don't make no trouble for us. Okay. Britney Spears has uh, never done no actual porn stuff. But people will pay lots of money and scholarships to watch digital creations of her doin' fake naughty stuff, heh. So, the nominees for pervert-guys-who-made-fake-porn-of-Britney-Spears-doin-stuff are: the claymation *Oops I Did Him Again* by Phallodough Productions; the digital photochop Pepsi Commercial: *If We Had Our Choice* by TeenCreams L.L.C.; and *Playing With My Micky Mouse Club* by SikNitWits. And the Ohyadewme goes to… *Oops I Did Him Again.*

(small blobs of PlayDough begin flying around the room; jaded laughter ensues)

Luvit: "And here to present The Big Ohh for the hottest porno out, please welcome RULDS? President, Hordin' MeWinky…"

Hordin': "Thank you Mikey, I mean Might. This year's

Big Ohh was no shot in the dark. We put all our wives together to come up with our flick pick to paint the walls with. After taxing my little temple with dozens of low-grade films, three titles of smut stuck out like a sore, red and swollen thumb. The nominees for this year's Big "Ohh" are: *Frequent Me*; *Shadow of a Vamp-whore*; and *Men of Boner*. Frankly, I don't care who gets the phallus; because as long as we're promoting procreation, we're winning the race."

Culture Shock: Plan 10

Was Brigham Young a sex-crazed alien from outer space? Who was his 28th wife? And what is the secret of the bees? These are not questions that merely pop into one's mind. But just because someone made them up doesn't mean they're not real.

The core staff at Wild Utah recently viewed the Sundance film "Plan 10 From Outer Space" on a suggestion from a friend. We're wondering if she wanted us to expand our perception of Mormon culture, or if she really wanted us to half lose our minds in one sitting. Reviewing this old flick may seem trite and cliché to some, but we feel there's a significant population here that don't know about it.

Plan 10 probably couldn't be classified as a "B movie" on its best day. But the story line is exceptionally creative. The plot begins with a very accurate portrayal of Mormon personality, the history of Salt Lake City, and the practices of the LDS Church. Things get weird when an LDS virgin named Lucinda finds random clues linking the pioneer Mormons to space aliens. Somehow, the whole space/planet concept doesn't come as a stretch to the viewer after Lucinda's dad and brother have a conversation about Mormon men getting their own planet after death.

The film seems to focus on the age-old controversy of literature. Can one small book make that much difference?

The Plan 10 (itself) exemplifies that it can. And after it stirs in inappropriate doses of wanton lust, cryptic flashbacks and a singing queen of planet Colab, it comes out of the oven incredibly bizarre.

Twice, the dialogue offers this parable:

"There are many truths. Some truths are uplifting, and some are not."

"How do you know which is which?"

"Well, the Church leaders tell me."

We wouldn't want to give away the story line because we feel this movie is an invaluable rendering of the Mormon faith. So was Brigham Young a sex-crazed alien from outer space? As it's put in the movie,

"It certainly would explain a lot about Salt Lake City."

Why Skiing Isn't Like Sex

Obviously, skiing is best when you're vertical... and alone. You smoke beforehand; then you put your clothes on.

Next you head outside. At this point, if you play with your equipment, it honestly won't help your performance.

Your bindings are to keep everything together, but they're by no means for anything kinky.

Now things get tricky. Of course, there is a certain amount of phallic symbolism to a ski, but remember also that skis are meant to bend. (And, you put wax on a ski to slide, but only in one direction.)

Once on the chairlift, you climb higher and higher, but the best part is coming down.

The snow is a thing of soft and sensual pleasure, but it's also very, very cold.

In skiing, the faster the better.

You try to go all day and sleep all night.

If you happen to catch air, you don't need to say excuse me.

But most importantly, all out of bounds chutes will be marked.

And why skiing is...

You begin carefully and slowly, as if to warm up and heed caution from injuries. As you ever so gradually pick up speed, cognition fades away.

You drop out, turn on and tune in. You can see what's going on and feel the terrain, but thinking turns to Zen. Endless repetition of direction change is a slow-motion exhilaration that is in no way monotonous.

Hot and cold; pleasure and pain; vigor and exhaustion all become one as the blood is rushing and cheeks are flushing. The physical tensions of wreathing and breathing stir into the mix and add to the wish that the run would never end.

Whew! I can't wait to get back up there.

But honestly, outerwear is key, and knowing how to handle ice is the total difference between a novice and an expert.

16

Mormon Liquor Laws

When non-drinkers make the laws, drinkers shake their heads.

1. Mormons must always have their garments on. If they need to take them off, they must put an arm or a leg part way into a clean pair before they can take the dirty ones off. This is where the liquor law came from which keeps drinkers from having two drinks in front of them at any one time. Garments are sacred; alcohol is evil.

2. Missionaries must always wear their nametags. This is where the server nametag rule comes from.

3. Every so often, any good Mormon has to re-up his Temple recommend status with the church; he pays his money, signs his name and viola! He's in. This is where the private club membership came from.

4. In Utah, you can only get one ounce of alcohol in a drink. You can't have one drop more than one ounce. This law seems to have come into play about the same time Mormons denounced plural marriage. "Trust me son, one's all you can handle."

5. You're not allowed to bring in alcohol from other states. This is much akin to a Mormon mission. A boy ventures out into the wilds of Wyoming; he is not allowed to consume alcohol or bring it back into the Motherland.

(Six) 3.2 is the most common type of beer in Utah. This is because it's the same number of children in each bedroom of a Mormon home.

7. Only a "worthy" Mormon is allowed to go into a Temple. In a restaurant, one cannot order alcohol unless he or she intends to order food. In light of the church, someone who orders food is "worthy" to drink alcohol.

8. Utah law mandates minimum markups on all alcohol sales. Anyone who knows the Church of Jesus Christ, Inc. certainly knows why.

9. Utah law allows people to brown bag liquor to dinner. Utah law prohibits brown eye for dinner, but people licker anyway.

10. Utah liquor laws were created by leaders who expect their flock to obey all laws set before them. These laws are widely ignored by alcohol consumers because there is nowhere else in the great-United States of America that tries so hard to enforce such ridiculous and unenforceable alcohol laws.

If the church enacted the current liquor laws, why didn't they enact the following:

1. Because we fear large bodies of water, no alcoholic beverage may be served in a vessel with a capacity larger than six (6) ounces.

2. Because we baptize the dead, it will be henceforth mandated that beer drinkers keep and store every empty

bottle of beer they consume for the rest of their lives.

3. Because we had no problem dispatching 120 men, women and children in the Mountain Meadows Massacre, we may from time to time spontaneously destroy every bit of alcohol in the state. If anyone tries to bring more alcohol in before we've calmed down from the slaughter, we may kill those people too.

4. Because drinkers don't have secret names or know the secret handshakes, anyone who wishes to order a drink must publicly yell out, "I'm the one called Fluffy!" Anyone who does not call out this phrase will not be given a drink.

5. Because we believe the Book of Mormon is the absolute truth without a shred of archeological evidence anywhere in the world, we bequeath onto drinkers the Liquor Law of Faith. All drinkers will be allowed one (1) alcoholic beverage per day. A drinker may consume this drink at any pace he or she desires. Then, the drinker must have faith and believe he or she has had all the intoxication needed for that day.

(By the way, let's all start ordering our drinks with the Fluffy method...)

PARKOPOLY

The game had not started fairly. Big Money rolled into town loaded with large portfolios and excellent liquidity. Molly Mo had an advantage also because she had known Summit and Wasatch counties much longer than the others had. The only advantage Snow Bum had was that he traveled light.

Big Money went first. His short roll landed him in Kamas. Big Money shook his head—declaring that he would not buy.

Molly Mo's turn followed. She rolled doubles, and chimed passed Big Money into Heber City. She quickly bought it and kept going. She rolled doubles again, strangely enough, and came all the way back to Payday. She collected her money, smiled, and sneaked that particular pair of dice back into her pocket.

Snow Bum picked up the "fair" dice and let them go. The dots counted six, which landed him on Racket Club Condos. Just when he was about to speak, Molly Mo perked up, "That's eight-hundred a month." Tragically confused about how she owned it without landing on it, Snow Bum split the rent and a day-old pizza with three other guys.

Big Money blew on the dice, but thought in his head that a hard worker makes his own luck. He tossed the dice, counted down the property spaces (sweating profusely) and found himself on Chance. Big Money picked up a card and read aloud. "Go directly to DeerCrest. Pay lender amount shown on card with Ritz-Carlton Hotel." He groaned and reluctantly signed over the inheritance from his Great-aunt Elaine.

Molly Mo's first doubles roll took her to Open Space. All three commenced in deep discussion on how to define the road, but it ended abruptly after Snow Bum's quip about consulting with Jack Kerouac. Again, Molly Mo lobbed the dice gently, and clicked down to Bear Hollow. She calmly tendered the cash to buy it.

Snow Bum's turn dropped him off just south of Price in Wellington, Utah on a Sunday afternoon. There he was stopped in an unconstitutional, non-resident traffic harvest and cited for numerous offenses. The two that bothered him most were Vehicular Deadhead Stickers, and Wearing Freaky Sunglasses in Our Conservative Little Town. They never even searched his VW Bus for marijuana...

Big Money was rarin' to buy. He flipped the dice over Snow Bum's VW, and slowly rolled through the properties in Deer Valley. Again and again, Big Money lost his count as he went over the experimental "Speed Hump." In stereo, the other two yelled, "Come on!" Big Money returned with, "I can't help it—the sexual innuendo's just too much."

Molly Mo rolled a high doubles. She sped passed the Jordanelle because she knew the devil lurked in large bodies of water. Excited with the pretense of landing on Wolf Creek Ranches, she took gleeful, high-lobbing steps. But the fixed dice did her wrong this turn, landing her on Peter Pan's

19

Smoke Shop on Park Avenue. Knowing that people wouldn't call the bongs "water pipes" after they left the store, she reached for her cell phone to call the police. She grit her teeth hard and pushed 'clear' when she couldn't remember the phone number to El Chubasco.

Snow Bum grabbed Molly's dice before she could sneak them away and pitched them down Kearns. He rolled doubles and landed on Rockport Ranches. Thinking it was a good deal, he coughed up the dough. When he read the property card, he realized that service from Utah Power and Questar was pretty indefinite. His second roll put him on Free Dog Crapping. There were signs at the borders of the property that read, "A man never stands so tall as when he stoops to pick up after his dog." As the other two watched intensely, Snow Bum knew he couldn't switch out for the real dice. He rolled Molly's loaded ones, and followed the Three-doubles rule to Out Of Work. He didn't really mind, though.

Big Money suggested that they throw that set of dice away and kick Molly off the Olympic committee. With money burning holes in his Armani suit, he rolled the dice, which coincidentally went doubles, and landed on Community Chest. He couldn't believe the luck when he read the card. "Buy a private gondola car at DeerCrest. Pay lender humorous and absurd amounts of money." The other two laughed and laughed. On his second roll, Big Money landed on 3.2 Beer. With Olympic venues on their way, he knew it was worth the battle to fight Utah's undying pseudo-Prohibition. But after knocking heads with Molly Mo for an hour, he looked over at Snow Bum who had cleverly started up a speakeasy.

After lots of ski town stories and three tall, nine-percent beers each, Big Money suggested quitting this game of Parkopoly and offered to take the other two up to the Rocky Mountain Chocolate Factory for a caramel apple.

Summit County Porn Regulations

"The soup that eats like the Starr Report"

The following is actual and/or paraphrased text taken from the Summit County Development Code for the construction of Adult-Oriented Businesses. I'm still wondering how a governmental committee was able to table these issues.

"An Adult Bookstore or Adult Video Store (is) a business establishment which, as one of its principle purposes, offers for sale or rental...visual representations which depict 'specified sexual activities' or 'specified anatomical areas,' or instruments, devices or paraphernalia which are designated for use...with specified sexual activities."

"Specified Sexual Activities means acts of masturbation, sexual intercourse, sodomy, ...fondling of the genitals or breast, ...flagellation or torture by or upon a person clad in undergarments, a mask or bizarre costume."

"Any material or performance is Obscene if patently offensive in the depiction of Nudity, sexual conduct, sexual excitement, sado-masochistic abuse or excretion."

"Semi-Nude: A state of dress in which a person wears opaque clothing covering...the genitals, pubic region, anus, ...the nipple and areola of the breast."

"Mandatory General Conditions... prohibit allowing a customer to masturbate in the presence of an employee."

"Mandatory General Conditions... prohibit allowing a patron to place any object within the person of any dancer, model, or performer."

Number of times each word was used in passage:

genitals 3
anus 3
areola 3
nipple 2
pubic 4
sodomy 3
masturbate 3
sado-masochistic 1
flagellation 1
torture 1
mask 1
excretion 1
incest 1
gonorrhea 1
syphilis 1
chlamydia 1

Stoner - The Lost Resort

(Commercial) Up in the Rocky Mountains on Highway 145, you can find a place called Stoner. At Stoner you can smoke 'till your lungs look like a bag of Kingsford, ski unkempt runs well after twilight, and crash free of charge in the lodge. But if you come, wear a really weird hat and bring your bag; because at Stoner, they don't take kindly to "normality," and they just don't take Amarijuan Disgust.

Marijuana Smokers - They're everywhere you want to go.

Everytime I drive past Stoner, my imagination frenzies. I'm a little twisted, but this is my image of Stoner in its days of operation...

All 37 of the season passholders roll out of bed feeling like total seeds. They limber up their joints and drag themselves to the bus stop. The door swings open, exhaling a thick Jamaican cloud. "Can-a-bus get me to Stoner?" the snowbums all ask in unison.

Once there, they rapidly spin up to the top. The egomaniacs come burning down through the blunts, trying to smoke their buddies. The jibbers all smurf a jib in the jib park; and the Mary Janes are totally cooking down the kind snow.

At lunch time, everyone heads in for the complimentary munchie bar. A waiter with bloody eyeballs might innocently ask, "Whhaat?" But lunch is finished quickly, because the good runs open in the P.M.

They all toke the big chair to the top of Green Dreams and traverse across Zig Zag. They drop down Log Jam (eschewing both Bushsmoker and See Forever Blurry) and come out on the toughest bump run on the mountain: Lost Lighter. Only the dopes dare drop down Paper Chute into the Pact Bowls. People are dying down there; and worse yet, passing out.

Ski School is very technical, and comprised of tie-dyed hippies. They're professional charlungs that insist there is only one right way to burn it up.

Of course, my description of Stoner's heyday might be a little off. But even so, with a name like that it was meant to go out. Even though they had the sponsorship of Gladbags, Visine and Doritos, they still weren't pulling in enough green. I bet the guys at the ticket window were always saying, "Oh ya...I forgot to charge that guy."

Dog Years Ahead

It is the year 2164. Many of the "futuristic" hopes and fears preconceived in the past millennium have materialized. Madonna is still making the pop charts, but she looks dreadful in a leather teddy. Human brains are now cybernetically upgraded at birth in order to wirelessly receive and process The Pipe—a cerebral-direct, superbandwidth information exchange, formally (and archaically) known as the Internet. Human bodies are showing mild signs of degeneration as mankind becomes increasingly more dependent on robotics and artificially intelligent decisions. And though man now possesses the awesome brainpower of instant, global thought processing, dogs are still what everyone is talking about.

Twenty-something years ago, a group of scientists developed an offbeat technology that allowed verbal communication between the sophisticated "Primates" and domestic Canines. As it turned out, opening the dialogue with a lessor species quickly came to be considered the greatest scientific feat of all time. It was especially impacting because dogs are just so damn cool.

Canines began to learn and soon became literate. They created schools of thought much like those of the ancient Greeks; and they started wearing sunglasses. Dogs became lovers of comedy and pranks, performed in plays and supporting Star Wars roles, and found great pleasure in art, intoxication and competition. And more than ever, they loved to pee on things.

Direct communication between the Primates and the Canines breathed all new life into the stereotype "Man's best friend." The trust they had shared in each other's eyes for thousands of years could finally be expressed in words. The relationship grew stronger, and in the course of only six years, the Canines found the right words to convince the Primates of letting them compete in the Olympic Games. (Since the dogs had no money or votes, their only course of action was begging)

The Summer Games of the LXVth Olympiad were held in 2152 in Buenos Aires, Argentina. The debut "BI-specie" event was the track & field addition of the 2+2 400-Meter Relay. Teams of two Primates and two Canines ran four, 100-meter legs, handing off a baton. All nations chose Greyhounds except the Republic of Antarctica (and having legalized heroine, it was little wonder). Eleven billion worldwide (and moon-colonized) processed the sites and sounds from The Pipe as the German team anchor-dog rocketed across the finish line to take the Gold. The precedent was set, and The Games would be changed forever.

The fascination with dogs has since overcome The Olympics. Every country of the world and two lunar republics send teams to the games, but Primates no longer compete. From overwhelming suggestions, a global forum and an instant opinion poll, the IOC reformed the athletic requirements in only four months to "Canine only;" dogs were faster, more athletic and much more exciting to watch. And with the recent innovation of the Puppy Patch, Canines became linked to The Pipe. Primates can now virtually race in the mind and senses of any Canine competitor, spectate from any position, or place bets with anyone in The Pipe.

This year the Summer Olympic Games are being held in Salt Lake City, Utah, host of the 2002 and 2068 Winter Games. A recent discovery of steroids has everyone worried. Oh—scratch that. Everyone just voted, and decided that performance-enhancing drugs will make these Olympic Games more exciting.

Micro is the Greyhound favored to win the long jump. The favorite for the Triple Marathon is the exhaustless Sheepdog from Greenland, Zuato. In dog fighting, the undefeated favorite drawing massive betting is a 210-pound Mastiff named Digger. Digger's so mean that he tore his owner's throat out last summer for reneging on a doggie treat. Tough luck.

The athletes are gearing up for the very popular but disgusting Ingestion Competitions. Everyone loves the "Last Dog to Vomit" event, and the fans are sure to chuckle and shake their heads at the newly added "Garbage Hoover" and "Toilet Quaff" events. Last week, Chaco the Amazing Labrador broke widespread laughter over The Pipe by proclaiming, "After I get a fresh Giardia booster, I'll drink anything!"

Tune in to these Olympic Games, and rejoice that there have been no expensive tickets to buy for over 100 years. Cheer for your favorite dog and place bets as you will; but remember: we are the masters of this domain. Keep it in your thoughts that dogs will always try to get more than they deserve. And if your favorite Canine craps in an inconvenient location, tell him or her to clean it up right away.

This message brought to you by Visa-Soft; it's everything you want your brain to be.

FILLMORE VIRGIN BEAVER, UTAH

Brian was HARDUP. It had been a TAD too long since he had tasted the SWEETS of female FRUITLAND.

He headed for LAYTON. He figured he could find a WILDCAT there whose MOUND CITY needed his LITTLE MOUNTAIN.

He met EDEN and the connection was STRONG. EDEN pretended to TEASDALE, but it was a BLUFF. She moved slowly toward Brian, then drew his face into the DELLE between her luscious KNOLLS.

Brian felt his JOHNSON WHIPUP from COTTONWOOD to OAK CITY. When EDEN felt this, she unfastened his BELT ROUTE, and NEELS down to give BRIAN HEAD.

It was PARADISE, but Brian knew it came at a PRICE. To return the favor, Brian followed THE AVENUES down to EDEN'S SUGARHOUSE. Expecting to encounter a GUSHER, he was surprised to find a DRY FORK. There was only one thing to do: NIBLEY.

Brian started in and almost immediately EDEN'S PLEASANT GROVE began to BLOOM. The RAINS came and so did EDEN, as she went from HONEYVILLE to RUSH VALLEY and back.

EDEN'S BASIN was as QUIGLEY as it could be, and Brian's DRAGON grew MAMMOTH. He started to MURRAY that if he didn't BUNKER soon, his WILDWOOD might explode.

Brian jerked EDEN beneath him in a forceful motion. He figured he needed a little HELPER, so he took one step back and started LA VERKIN—his CASTLE ROCK pulsed in deep VERMILLION.

Brian estimated the ANGLE and headed straight for BONE VALLEY. When Brian got DOWNTOWN, the JOY of it was almost too much for EDEN. She began to MONA, then she cried, "MOORE, MOORE, MOORE!"

The event became a HURRICANE, as it went from ALTA to ESCALANTE in no time at all. Brian continued to drive his TEMPLE into BONNEVILLE, and EDEN traversed in her CANYONS until the final moment when they both screamed, "EUREKA!"

The PAYSON was BOUNTIFUL, so Brian and EDEN toweled off and lit up a SALEM.

The Utah Way

Take a drive over to Colorado. If you get out of your car in the very largest, most remote mountains and walk deep into some canyons, you'll find places where the ignorant, old miners screwed up the land—then left a bunch of shit laying around for no one to pick up.

Ya, it's offensive, but it's nothing like what we have here in Utah. Most of Colorado's nasty stuff is out of the general view shed.

The Great Wall of China can be seen from space; so can The Great Pyramid. But there's nothing great about seeing the Kennecot Copper Mine from space. It's the epitome of raping and pillaging the land. So what if somebody made a gajillion dollars on it. It's ugly, gross and disgusting, and from an intellectual's perspective, maybe it could have been mined in a way not so visible from Salt Lake.

But wait, there's more! With your view of the Kennocot Mine, you'll receive the shitty looking mine by Woods Cross, Harper's crappy quarry just into Parley's Canyon, and the wretched stench of one super-polluted Utah Lake. And that's not all! At no additional cost, you'll get the horrid looking rock quarries creeping up Browns Canyon Road, the public rape of Wasatch County also known as DeerCrest, the unsettling industry of water pipes, electric lines and whatever-the-hell traversing Provo Canyon, AND the insidi-

ous MagCorp. on the Great Salt Lake.

Yes, this state's motto is "Industry." And it's amazing just how bad a scant 1.4 million people want to fuck this place up. What's a little high-radiation nuclear waste to throw into the mix? So what if your kids are drinking excessive levels of arsenic and mercury. Let's make money! Let's get rich and kill absolutely dead one of the most naturally beautiful places on earth.

If you want to make money, just charge a fee to have excavators dump endless loads of garbage, fill dirt and tailings on your ranch in Eastern Summit County! The local government won't get in your way. While we're at it, why don't we all start strip mining the entire Wasatch Range? There's gotta be more good stuff to sell that we haven't found yet! Let's keep drilling for oil in the Uinta Basin—even though 99.8 percent of the wells don't produce shit.

Let's build one more huge, offensive highway, develop every square inch of land around it and label it a "Legacy" so that 12 greaseball Mormons can make their next gajillion. Hell, they've earned it. They deserve to be paid a million dollars for every acre of land they can piss on. We don't need a bullet train. That's for the faggy, San Francisco intellectuals. It doesn't make nearly the money a Legacy Highway can.

Maybe, just maybe…if we industrialize with no thought of sustainability or future consequences…we can build the state of Utah into one gigantic city. Ten million babies can scream beneath the smoggy ecstasy of a metal grinding, gay-ridden, one religion high-rise mega-metropolis where brainwashed beta-humans sing songs about Moroni as they toil for the greater good. Provo will arise as the new spiritual center. The suburb of Moab can be the nuclear production and plutonium waste dump. Tithing will go up 12 percent, and The Church will buy up Detroit, OPEC and eventually the rest of the world—tax-free. Ahhhhh... That sounds reeeal good. Shhhhewwwww...

Sorry Selwyn. That ain't gonna' happen.

28

The Overtake of Planet Vote

Not knowing how things end is a common neurosis among Utah folk. While the residents of Park City were mostly monosyllabic, they somehow knew what was going to happen.

You see, it all started at a time when Planet Vote was uninhabited. A small but hearty cocoon of migrant Gopmos dropped unexpectedly into a protected dale. There, the fruits of life were plentiful. The swath of Gopmos procreated and evolved into a nesting, predatory species, much akin to insects.

The Gopmos' Nest began to grow rapidly through tight-knit networking, and by its vulgarly excessive reproduction. The swarm was kept well-fed with the capture and consumption of nomadic rogues. But one day, an alien species had the speed to escape apprehension. It returned home to relay the message of this bountiful new world. Soon, more of these aliens were dropping into the dale to prospect its fertility. One particular set decided the plateau above the dale was highly desirable for living—especially given its suitably frigid temperatures and delicious beer.

The predatory Gopmos grew larger and larger. With its increased appetite, the Nest no longer found satisfaction in the consumption of rogue migrants, and paused hungrily with greed. The Nest's council of lords gave orders to execute a scheme for seizing larger prey. The dutiful worker-drones crafted a much larger trap, and baited it heavily with money and scholarships and wonderful vacations.

Soon after the trap was prepared, a giant traveling Ioc was drawn not only to the free shit, but the icy temperatures on the plateau. When it became ensnared, the council regrouped. Without knowledge of how much larger a prey they could get, they resolved to dangle the Ioc as bait to net an even larger prize.

Thousands of rogue migrants were drawn to the bait. While the Gopmos' Nest waited patiently for the bigger fish, it regarded all the inbound traffic as insignificant. Many of these small nomads were related to the much larger Ioc, and built small colonies of their own adjacent to the cold climates.

The predatory Gopmos surveyed the sky in gluttonous hunger. Free of their attention, the eclectic new residents began to cooperate, and composed themselves as the Nomos. The Nomos were not entirely happy with the predators' government of such things as the consumption and advertising of delicious beer. They worked together to cut away at the roots of the Gopmos' Nest. This exposed the Gopmos' vulnerable young, and weakened the network of the swarm.

In a single, massive vote, the cooperating Nomos darkhorses dashed the core of the Nest, severing it from its stronghold on the land, and sent it hurling into the wicked depths of Nevada.

OK, I lied. The Park City residents weren't exactly monosyllabic. They drank beer, and made art—and that has made all the difference.

29

Money (in marketing epitaph)

John's dad left him his money,
His grandpa left his dad all his dough.
And so on through the family tree
The family mullah did go.
Now John leaves all of his kids
Sacks of cash as you know that he should
Cause it's true with a name like Smuckers,
It certainly has to be good.

Sam spent his on the number seven
Lost at life, luck land him in heaven.
He now looks down on the Vegas strip
And relishes betting, cash and chip.
Oh, what he'd give for neon light
And a chance to make it a blockbuster night.

Here lies Sally,
without a doubt,
her ship had come in
but the truck backed out.
It was red as can be
and strangest of things—
shaped like a bull,
Red bull gives you wings.

I started with none
And built up a ton
"You want it,"
says my psyche.

It's buried with me,
and deadly traps three,
You say,
He likes it, hey Mikey.

To Mary's priest, she made daily confession.
(Prostitution was her chosen profession)
She had, as they say, money to blow,
Nightly she sold a honey of an ohhh.

adios and hasta nunca
we spit on the sangre de Bill
por lying and cheating y stealing
a man made his sangre spill
this mundo takes its dinero back
Bill rapidamente to hell
siempre he'll starve and think to
himself, Yo quiero taco bell

This dreamer dreamt a life of grand
Then grasped it in his weakened hand
To meet the mark he worked and planned
With many years of hardship spanned
This story may seem so far trite
But listen to his self-made blight:
In times when debts grew great in height
He sold his blood to keep things tight
At forty bucks a bleedin' pop
The years did yield a vampire's crop
And funded success at his health's lop
The guy was good to the last drop.

Local Rednecks Kick Butt in Ford's Sport Trac Challenge

Y'all don't know who the Children of the Wasatch are, but them's four kin we can all be proud of. Not long ago, the Kin flew on one of them jet airplanes to the White Mountains in New Hampshire to compete in Ford's fancy big Sport Trac Challenge. Sponsored only by Bad Ass Coffee of Park City, Dustin Sturges, Scott Wilson, Jaima Anderson and Tony Larson tore it up somethin fierce skiing, kayaking, climbing, and mountain biking against real professional athletes who had sponsorships like K2, Outside Magazine, and Ford.

The Kin landed in New Hampshire on a Friday. They were greeted by some Ford folks, and given a shiny new, Ford Sport Trac pickup truck. It was real perty, and the Ford folks were probly a tad concerned about just handin the keys over to a group of 24-year-olds like Team Wasatch.

Now we love a good Ford truck, but the Kin said they got in this four-door spaceship and it had one of them global PMS navigation systems—and the dang thing started talkin to 'em! Team Wasatch checked in with the officials, barely made it through the orientation, then headed directly to a nearby tavern.

"I figure you should race the way you train; get loaded, go out and ski the next day," professed Team Captain Dustin Sturges. So the Wasatch Kin, sturdy with sea level oxygen, trained well into the night. After a few dozen drinks, a carnage of hand-rolled cigarettes and a refreshin' two hour sleep, the team awoke and fired up for Sturges' 7 a.m. start time in the backcountry ski event. Sturges competed hard and finished a respectable second place. With lungs that look like bags of Kingsford charcoal, he couldn't quite overcome professional Luke Miller.

Scott Wilson on the other hand weren't even dewy-eyed over the previous night's session. He came out and whooped some kayaking ass, taking first place by over a minute and a half (that's a long time in dog years and in kayakin'). The Wasatch Kin were in second place at the end of the day—and it was getting prit-near obvious that these games were rigged. While Wilson's second place finisher was only behind him by 44 points, Sturges' second place put him 140 points behind Luke Miller. The backcountry skiing would be the only event with such a spread, and dammit if itwernt more than the Kin could overcome.

The climbing and biking events wern't 'til Sunday, so another night of honky-tonkin was in the cards. Good and pissed-off about Ford's dirty, stinkin, yella-bellied scoring system, Team Wasatch decided it was time for some real fun. The Kin found an open dirt parking lot, punched the gas and cranked out a few donuts in that new truck. Sturges, a trained stunt driver, started feelin' like the Duke Boys. He spun some good ones, then dropped team members Tony Larson and

31

Jaima Anderson off at the lodge. Then he thought he'd give'er another go.

"We were actually sober, we just decided to spin some donuts," Sturges said. "I decided to do one more; the front tire popped and the truck just flopped over on its side. It was those damn horrible Firestone tires." Our guess is that it was probly not so much the arrow as the Indian.

Because of the accident, Sturges was denied any prizes for his second place finish and $2000 was deducted from the team's winnings for truck repair. The team took the misfortune in stride and just felt lucky for the comp'ed tickets and fancy hotel accommodations for the event. "At least they didn't kick us out of the competition," Sturges praised.

The final day started with the climbing competition and a knee-slappin performance by Jaima Anderson. Again, it was obvious this thing was rigged. Anderson schooled all three of the boys, but was only given second place. Ed Crossland was awarded first place, even though everyone saw this bubba pull on every fricken piece of gear, including the cameraman's rope.

Tony Larson was the final Wasatch competitor in the mountain biking. He rode dang hard to third place behind a beastly competitor that the others affectionately called the android. Pete Swenson is ten foot tall if he's an inch, with legs of steel and eyes that can pierce your very soul. Swenson took a nasty digger right out of the start gate, spent six-minutes fixing a flat tire, and still lapped all three of the other competitors on the three-mile course.

"I think we had one hell of a showing for doing 12oz curls and chain smoking cigarettes on the Colorado River two weeks before the competition," Sturges said.

So four Utah rednecks (sponsored by Bad Ass) go up against three other teams of professional athletes. The Utahans drink and smoke, roll a truck, and they still whipped all their asses. The stats for the competition can be found on that Internet that everybody's talkin about. Go to www.sport-tracchallenge.com, and click on the "White Mountains." There you can see that the Children of the Wasatch weren't too far off first place; and if the yella, milquetoast-coward judges of the Sport Trac Challenge wouldna rigged it, we think the Wasatch Kin woulda won.

(Editor's note: this story was run June 7, 2000—four days before the first fatal Firestone tread separation. We thought Dustin was crazy for saying the rollover was the tire's fault).

The Plight of PSIA

How many skiers does it take to screw in a light bulb? 201. One PSIA director to sit in the dark, 199 Professional Ski Instructors of America to kiss his ass, and one rad som'bitch to make all the turns.

But don't get me wrong. Some of my best friends are PSIA. And if you talk to them, they'll probably tell you jokes I haven't heard yet.

If you've spent any time around the industry, you may have heard these alternative definitions of PSIA:

Pretty Skiing – Inadequate Ability
(backward) Assholes In Stretch Pants

But don't get me wrong—those aren't mine; These are mine:

Pushing Skiing's Industry Apparel
Pansies Skipping In Arrogance
Pretty Sure I'm Awkward
Perfect Skidding If Anything
Professionally Slow Ice Avoiders
Position Sacred Indicates Asskissing

Parabolic Skis – Idiotic Actions
Powder Scared, Incline Averted
Putrid Skiboot-infusing Aroma
Put Simply, Isn't Alpine
Pole Stuck In Ass
Potent Snowplows, Impotent Athletes
Pigs Skating In Analogy
Patio Skilled Inebriated Alcoholics
Panty Shield Ideal Advertisements
Prattles & Spits in Arguments
Poops Shorts in Avalanches
Posing Self-important Instruction Amateurs
Psychologically Skewed Identity Anxieties
Picabo's Salivating Interest Attempts
Putting Spam Into Action
Profoundly states, "I'm Awesome"

Survivor

After four years of college, and a serious mental break-down, I applied to 11 ski schools in the western United States for the 94-95 winter season. I received information by mail on the hiring clinics at all the big Colorado resorts, and a handful of other places like Mammoth and Big Sky. I picked Telluride, Colorado because it seemed, by far, the strangest.

I had managed to save about $150, and after I hocked my last few valuable items, I had a little over $350. I sent Telluride resort a cashier's check for $80 for the hiring clinic, and looked at the map to figure out how close I could get on a Greyhound bus. The bus line through southwest Colorado had a stop in Ouray, which was only 12 miles from Telluride. I figured 12 miles was no big deal, so I bought a one-way ticket from Grand Rapids, Michigan to Ouray, Colorado.

Assets: After the bus ticket, I had $125 dollars, a bag of clothes, a bag of ski equipment, two Tylenol with Codeine, and almost 20 ham and turkey sandwiches that Gram packed into my little carry-on bag.

Liabilities: With not a nickel more than $125, I was moving to a place I had never been, with no job, no place to stay, and where I knew no one. I could not ask anybody for more money, and I wouldn't out of the little pride that I had left. I said my good-byes, and had my beloved grandparents drop me off at the bus stop.

On the trip out, I had to change busses three times. Each bus stopped in every little podunk town along the way. On the longest leg (Chicago to Denver) I made a friend, and we took the Codeine together. When other passengers got hungry, I started selling them sandwiches—high as a kite on Codeine.

On the Denver to Grand Junction leg, I remember going through Summit County, Colorado, then passing Vail. I admired the ski town Christmas lights reflecting off the snow as we chugged through late that night.

On the last bus, the sun started coming up just out of Junction. I couldn't believe my eyes. The mountains were gone. All I could see was baron dessert—something I'd never seen before. I remember the horrific feeling that I'd made a huge mistake. What if Telluride was a tiny little ski area in the middle of nowhere?

Then the bus came out of the other side of Montrose. The San Juan Mountains of southwest Colorado shot up into the sky like the Swiss Alps. I'd skied the Alps, and these mountains were no tough comparison.

Twenty minutes later, the bus tootled through a little town called Ridgway. The bus driver and I were fascinated with giant herds of deer and elk on both sides of the road. I glanced briefly to the right side and saw a little road sign with an arrow that read "Telluride." For one hell-raising nanosecond, I thought about screaming to stop the bus. But I didn't.

The bus dropped me off in the amazing town of Ouray. The mountains were absolutely huge, and at 6 a.m., it was damn cold. I stood on a corner and hitchhiked for about 10 minutes; but there was almost no traffic, and I was freezing my ass off. After 40 hours of nausea due to extreme nervousness, I figured it would be worth it to drop some of that $125 (plus $12 for sandwiches) on a little hot breakfast. I ate really slowly, and started talking to people to see who might be nice enough to drive me that 12 miles over to Telluride.

This little skinny guy piped up; "I'll drive you over there for forty bucks."

What is this, I thought, the land of the criminally insane? I was out to make friends, so I asked questions politely. Came to find out that Telluride was 12 miles as the crow flies, but that there's a 14,000 foot mountain between there and Ouray. The shortest way to Telluride by car was 65 miles.

I tried freeze-yer-ass-off hitchhiking again, but that didn't work. There seemed few alternatives, so I went back in the breakfast place and agreed. The ride over was beautiful, and the guy pointed out Sneffels—the snowcapped fourteener that wasn't on my Michigan road atlas.

An hour later, we pulled into Telluride. I asked the guy if he knew a cheap hotel. He told me there's no such thing in Telluride, but that the Oak Street Inn was the cheapest in town.

I anted up $40 for the ride, and checked into a European style room (with a common bathroom for each floor) at Oak Street for $40; I went from $127 to $47, and reality hit me like the brick I had just dropped in my shorts. The truth was, I was one night and one bowl of rice away from being dead broke and out of the game.

I wouldn't start the ski instructor college until the next morning; so let's just say that I spent the entire day laying in the hotel room freaking out. I almost called my mom, but couldn't bring myself to do it.

I awoke the next day with only one thought—TIME TO MAKE MY NEW BEST FRIEND. I geared up, and headed over to the bottom of Coonskin lift where I would meet the Telluride Ski Instructors. About one hundred feet from the lift, a guy popped out of his house, all geared up and heading the same direction as me. The mountain was closed, so I knew where he was going. We introduced ourselves, and I decided "Rob" was my guy.

When we got to the lift, there were about 100 people who I liked to believe were all in the same boat I was. We were separated into groups by ski credentials.

I put on a good show for my clinician, ate the remainder of Gram's sandwiches for lunch and met some great guys—one who told me he was in a similar position 20 years ago, and that he would put me up if I could wait a few days. I tried to find Rob after we came off the mountain, but he wasn't around.

Around 6 p.m., I headed over to Eddie McStiff's for a $3.00 slice of pizza and a $3.00 beer. When I got back to the hotel, I ponied up another $40 for my room (leaving me with a handful of change).

Late that night, I met some construction workers in the "TV room." They offered me some wine from three giant jugs. I thought about the movie Animal House. I decided there was only one thing I could do: I got drunk fast— Telluride's altitude of 8750 gave me the tolerance of a high school freshman.

I got talking with these guys, and one said he really wanted to ski. I told him that I had an extra pair of skis and an extra pair of boots that I would sell to him real cheap. He was interested; I was ecstatic. I showed him the gear, told him what it was really worth, and gave the guy a bargain at $225.00. Cha-ching!

I felt like a rich man. And the next morning, I ran into Rob again. He told me HE was out of money, but if I bought the food, I could stay for a while. Seemed like a beautiful symbiosis.

That afternoon, a Serbian guy named Neb moved into Rob's house as well. He had a van with over $100,000 of alcohol in it. When Rob and I got off the snow, I remember sitting in his hot tub, sipping Pear William (my favorite liqueur). I was entranced with the views of the San Juans, and giggling about how nervous I had been the previous four days.

I started working on Telluride's race department days later. A week after I moved in, Rob kicked me out because his girlfriend was coming in from California. The guy from my clinic, Ken, drove down to Rob's and picked me up with all my shit. He and his wife graciously gave me my own room with my own bathroom, took me out or cooked me dinner a humiliating number of times, and gave me free run of their house.

I stayed with Ken for almost five weeks, then rented a teeny little studio with another ski bum named Matt.

I made it.

Telluride was the most fun I've ever had in my life. I moved away almost two years later with a girlfriend, a U-Haul full of shit, and a cat.

Pow Mow Brown Cow

Instead of producing issue 19 of Wild Utah like we were supposed to last Sunday, Andy and I jumped in the Isuzu Growler and headed up north. The fact that we needed to finally make some turns together counted less than tertiary to the dozens of other reasons why we skipped an extra week of Wild Utah.

It had been about seven days since that 50-inch, late February storm blanketed the Wasatch, so we weren't counting on freshies. Powder Mountain's website hadn't been updated since the previous Thursday, but SKI UTAH's snow report showed Pow Mow with 114-inch base and "real powder." Needless to say, that was exciting.

The drive up was awesome. We took I-80 to I-84, then around the loop at Pineview Reservoir. The mountains in those parts are absolutely huge and scenic. Armed only with a caffeine buzz, we came unglued as we rounded the lake and putted through the town of Eden.

It was no short drive. We didn't leave Park City until 9:10; so by the time we got to Eden at 10:20, we were certainly ready to ski. It was still another steep, 20-minute chug up Powder Mountain Road to reach the resort. The Growler needed second gear for the whole climb. Though the canyon was beautifully draped with poached ski-lines, it was suspiciously deserted. We saw no skiers, and counted only three cars on the lengthy Powder Mountain road.

When we reached the resort, we were excited to see only about 50 cars in the main lot. We booted up, met Mark Paulsen, and legalized our lift access. Mark recommended Lightning Ridge and Cobabe Canyon for the best snow. When we asked about "real powder," he said he had done his part to track it all out, and that there "really wasn't any left."

At 10:45, we were on the Sundown lift. No lines, no people. From the top, an unbuckled slide to the right brought us to the Lightning Ridge waiting area. Here, a cat was supposed to drag us up to the top. Instead, a young, hotdog (named Mark) came blasting down on a utility snowmobile. I laughed thinking about the 'bile speed limit at Park City Mountain.

Mark pulled us up to the top of the ridge with the throttle at full. Insurance nightmare. I was imaging being pulled by the cat. Once at the top, Mark directed us down the ridge to "ski down, then traverse, ski down, traverse..." Once he whipped around and sped off, we side-slipped over the wind-scoured crust to a hidden spot out of the wind. As they say, out of sight, out of mind.

Once the proper state of mind was reached, we buckled up and did as both Mark's told us to do. You can tell how good the skiing is by how spoiled the locals are. On the first pitch, we skied barely-tracked powder all the way down into the canyon—the kind of snow you see on Jupiter at 10:30 a.m. on a powder day. All tracked out, huh? We traversed back onto the ridge, and came down through yet more powder. The conditions were deep everywhere; knee deep Styrofoam, to cappuccino foam, to "real powder." We were high as a kite.

Further down the ridge, we looked back up to see massive rock cliffs and boulders. There were chutes of all varieties and just the kind of insanity we were looking for.

We rounded the point at the bottom to NOT stand in line for the Paradise lift. Two minutes into the ride, we discussed how this lift was aptly named. The entire ridge beneath the lift was one gigantic whale spine of a natural terrain park. The red rock boulders and cliffs just kept coming, topped with massive tufts of the 114-inch base. Any size drop you're man enough for lies beneath the Paradise lift. Andy and I wanted to jump off sooo bad.

I thought of the masses of people and endless lift lines at Park City and Snowbird. Holy shit was this going to be some kind of day.

We unloaded and quickly snipped down through the mildly bumped-out "Strait Shot" onto our whale spine. No one was in the way, and barely anyone was on the lift to watch us go big. We skied a perfect looking chute to access more of what we wanted. My first hop turn didn't go so well, as the snow had been baking in the sun for days. I figured for cush, but it was rock hard; my skis shot forward and I sat down on the couch. OK. Variable conditions.

We took our first trip through the spine somewhat tentatively. No need to smash bones against rock because we didn't know what to expect. It was still outrageous. The second run allowed for a bit more irrationality. I went somewhat grande, dropping a few five to tens; Andy went venti, with packs of wild boarders hootin' at him from the lift. All skiable lines were incredibly vacant and the landings were pleasingly soft.

It didn't take much of this stuff to work up some hunger, so we headed toward the Hidden Lake lodge. This was where most of the tourists were skiing, but still no lift lines. Without caring what the resort called it, about halfway up this ridiculously slow lift we renamed it the "Fuck This Express." My feet were hurting, but the lift just never seemed to end.

Once at the top, the Hidden Lake Lodge looked amazingly like a government building. Brick, stark and without style. The menu was short and pretty pathetic—nothing remotely healthy. (Unlike Brighton, they do take plastic) I grabbed a deep-fried chicken sandwich and headed upstairs. The 360-degree views on the upper level are breathtaking; but you get your breath right back when you see that the tables are all crafted of construction-grade, OSB plywood. When we were finished, we glanced over at the trashcan, then down at our mess, and decided "they do not have people for this."

We skied hard the rest of the afternoon. We took numerous rides up Paradise and Lightning Ridge, still finding deep, spaciously tracked foam on every line. Afterward, we hung out in the Powder Keg bar and talked a long time with the employees. That was as fun as anything else.

These things do not exist anymore: undiscovered mom and pop ski resorts with no high-speed lifts and outrageous terrain; lift tickets so cheap and you tip the bartender $20 for a beer; Rocky Mountain weekend skiing with NO (none, zero, these-guys-can't-even-pay-the-electric-bills) LIFTLINES.

Powder Mountain is not a destination resort. It's the kind of place where the employees abide by no corporate policies. It's the kind of place where ski lessons cost $35—with rentals!!! It's the kind of place where bartenders wear WHATEVER they want, keep baby food in the beer cooler, and burn the shit out of your burger while they're talking to you.

On weekends, no one is there. On weekdays, the only cars in the lot are owned by employees. When we were there, Powder Mountain had almost 20 more inches of base than any of the other ski resorts. It's just unbelievable.

Any day you want to get out to ski, take off at any time in the morning—don't worry about how long it takes to get there—and head up to Powder Mountain. There will be better snow and fewer skiers than anywhere else in the Wasatch. And if you've been around a while, Powder Mountain might just remind you of what skiing was like 20 years ago.

Talk of the town clown

Well, the ski season really seems to be winding down to the end. Soon it will be time for mud, time for early-season dog feces to thaw, and the annual flux of Park City residents. Two young women living on Woodside, **Sharon Aroom** and **Cheryl Yershit** claim, "We hate each other, and now we just want to go home." And who could blame them. With next-door neighbors like **Ralph Hard** and **Heath Rewup**, who needs to live where steam cleaners dare not to go?

Meanwhile up at Silver Lake, the uniquely vague couple, **Herm Afrodite** and **Ann Droginous** have announced they are to be married in September. We would suggest that they name their first child **Pat**, but that would be assuming gender.

Some ladies were laughed out of a certain bar for wearing furs; not only was **Luke Adat** heckling, but **Ida Dunnit** too. What a shame.

We look forward to the upcoming Park City Town Games to take place this summer. It's gonna be a knock-down, drag-out competition between the **Oldtown Patchoulis** and the **Park Meadows Richpeople**. Park Meadows seems like it won't have a chance in the BCASTYB—the Bar Crawl And Stumble To yer Bed; not with fierce Oldtown competitors like **Amanda Merthanme**, **Buddy Diddit**. Then again, the Richpeople have the corporate tug all wrapped up with **Irene Eggoshiate** and **Helen Wheels**. Good luck to all.

Now did ya'll check out who was together at the highschool spaghetti dinner? **Minnie Skert** and **Les Izmore** were clinging like beginners downloading Townlift. The kids were great, but have we ever heard of Noxema? The word "zits" doesn't even describe kids like **Ward Ovchicks** and **Frank Lee Ugly**. And I'd say **Wanda Howmutch** was wearing just a tad too much makeup.

The gossip is flying after the scandal between **Hugh G. Rection** and **Connie Lingus**. **Skip Foreplay** would not comment after he received counseling from his lawyer, **Jack Mahogoff**; but **Barry Dabone** let it fly to **Mike Hunt**, our inside source. Further information to be disclosed tomorrow by **Mark Mywerds**.

We would like to salute the Park City Fraternity **Choppa Choppa Gramma** for their ongoing efforts. May the winds of fortune blow back your way.

And to the other phat frat, **Gotta Bagta Sel**: we congratulate **Cecil O'Cybin** and **R. Yewhl** on their recent finish of the Boston Marathon. Nice work boys.

We were sorry to see parking citations issued to **Norm Alday** and **Sam Alchit,** but you know guys, you have to play by the rules

A Farewell To Snow

Sure, Snowbird's still open, but skiing and boarding are off the radar screen. Although it doesn't really seem like we got that much more snow than last year, we've heard a lot fewer bellyaches about it. Hmmm...

The truth of the matter is the way one ends a season is almost as important as the season itself. What will you take with you on that long journey through the summer? What is your last popcorn kernel of skiing to savor while you know you won't taste it again until next fall?

Well, Clown Day is a good way to begin to kiss off the season. But if you really want to do it right, you'll need some sort of skis, and you'll need to be at the closing day for Alta.

I write about closing day at Alta with a beer in my hand; and it takes me back. At Alta, the snow is almost always good. Sure, there's a bit more attitude there than most other ski resorts... in the world—which is considerable when you shake your head at the attitude anywhere else—but Alta, sweet, sweet Alta is the Way to say goodbye.

On April 22nd, the powder was fresh. That recent 60-inch dump left a terrific base of Styrofoam for a new 8-10 of fresh to fall upon. That's nice for some mind-baked runs of bliss in the morning, but hey, let's not work too hard here. Tailgating starts around 10 a.m. Superheroes, ballerinas, and chicks dressed up as buffaloes really get going around noon. After lunch and what pours into the afternoon is beer and other stuff. People get noisy. Things get rowdy. Then around 3:30, droves begin to exodus up Germania. If I were to throw an average at it, I'd say at least 3-6 beers per person make the trip.

Everybody knows that Alta's olda thanya sista. Slow lifts, deep snow, and traversing are what it's all about. Well, just before closing, nobody's thinking about skiing. So they ride up slowly, then traverse.

High Russell (or HighBoy as the locals it) is the place. It's a scant little ridge above 2000 feet of vertical seriousness. On top, no one's serious. Lighters burn and pass. Beer and Jack Daniels pour without cups. Intoxication is rife and people are dressed up like butterflies and cowboys.

At 4:20, the ski patrol informs the crowd of several hundred that the area is officially closed for the season; then they ski away. Liability transferred. Party on Wayne.

Sobriety is no longer common. But you're at Alta.

The wind is blowing a steady 40-mph and gusting around 60. It's snowing hard, but the sun teases the crowd with several small donuts of blue sky.

Hang out for a while. Have some laughs. Cause if you try to ski down, everyone will throw snowballs at you.

Goodbye Snake Creek, Honeycomb and Thunder. Goodnight John Paul, Beaver and Paradise. See ya next year Empire, Jupe and 9990. This kids got 2000 feet of Germania to go. It ain't flat, and I ain't sober.

43

I.R.S.ex Instructions

1a.   To begin preparation for filing, first take the Relationship Test: If you are single, you will not need to plan. If you are married, plan 10 minutes of preparation for every year married.

1b. If married, estimated spousal relief can be calculated by taking the residual interest in each other's figures and subtracting the number of dependent children.

2a. Once the joint interest condition is met, frivolous name change may increase the total return. Example: Nurse Ratchet, Master, Queen Lashing, naughty little boy.

2b. Other alternative labels can be calculated. These false circumstances may also raise the aggregate: Playing student/professor, Tax Collector, Tarzan/Jane.

3a. By this point, the capital number should be gaining. After using the Peel-Off label, this item can be examined as "ordinary," "standard," or "inflated." Estimating smallest contributions or actual tips will result in lump-sum losses and extensive penalties.

3b. The capital number can take the EIC (Exaggerated Inches Credit) and enter it on line Y. Its statutory installment has endless legal repercussions, so both filers should understand their responsibilities.

3c. The head of household should immediately begin to schedule breakfast, sweet nothings and flowers in his mind to avoid any future deductions.

4a. With filing well under way, miscellaneous forms are crucial to the investment for a positive return. Methods should be adjusted frequently. Spontaneous rollovers will put the right figure on top, and optimally align each filer's contributions. (As usual, there is a penalty for early withdrawal)

4b.   With form XX divided zealously by the capital number, and individual contribution rates joined harmoniously, the taxing will continue to gain. The combined rate will increase rapidly until a final balloon payment is distributed "with integrity and fairness to all."

5a.   At this point, recoveries can be made—with one exception: if spousal relief is not received, the amount you owe should be obvious.

5b. Were you covered? If distributions were not covered, you may qualify for New Child Tax credits next year.

Why The Hell Would You Want To Build A House?

OK, so you're an idiot and you want to build a house. Let's skip the "buy property," "find a loan" and "choose a competent architect" bullshit and move right into the painful, rectal itch of construction.

You've nailed down your construction plans and know unequivocally what you want to build; you have a construction budget so you can dole out monies in precise, controlled amounts. (You didn't forget a sizable sum for "General Allowance" or "the unforeseen," right)?

I'll tell you right now—the gospel of construction is to take your FINALIZED schedule and budget, then add three months & 30 percent. Don't believe me? Fine. You don't have to listen. But in the end, that's where you'll be.

OK, smart guy, let's build.

Water: If you don't have it, you don't even get to start. (tack on as much time as it takes)

Site Prep: You're gonna have to put up a stupid little "erosion control" fence to keep any wild-ass balls of dirt from running away. You'll also need an LOD fence or "limit of disturbance." Both are small tasks, but your friendly, government inspector will bust your ass for either.

Excavation: You're building in Utah. Sorry. It's not like digging in a sandbox half-full of cat shit. The good news is you may never have to worry about your house settling; the smack on the ass is you might have to spend an extra $10,000 to blast the hole open with dynamite. (please see "General Allowance" above)

Footings and Foundation: Heh. Even some of the most reputable concrete guys around can screw it up big time. Be sure to keep the concrete from freezing, the top of the wall level, and the concrete plant paid (some guys take your money, but don't pay the plant; can you say lien?). If any of these don't go right, count on spending more. (please see "General Allowance" above)

Framing: Assuming your concrete came out all right, your framing should be rapid and exciting. Visibly, things begin to happen as shit starts goin' vertical. If it's cold, your guys won't work and neither will their nail guns. This price should be set in stone in a contract; but don't be surprised if lumber prices go up 20 percent and you spend more than you anticipated. (please see above)

Dry-In: This is merely getting windows hung and a waterproof material over the roof sheathing. Guess what—some of your windows are going to break. If you use felt and leave it to blow in the Utah wind, some of it will tear up; you'll spend dollars to fix it. If you cover with bituthane, you spend good money, but get a great dry-in.

Electric, Plumbing, Heating: This is the longest and most ass-chafing part of the project. Making sure all the kids are playing nice with each other is tough. Especially since you figure out that your "perfect" design concept doesn't work in five rooms, and you have to have them redrawn by the architect...which costs more money. You'll also have to either pay the General for change orders (get them all in writing you idiot!) and/or any subcontractor affected. This is also the point that the General and/or subs decree that your plans suck and are missing all kinds of details. This will delay the job substantially. (please see "add three months")

Four-way: No, this is not a sexual fantasy. You're in deep shit. Four-ways don't often pass the first inspection. Why? Your rough framing, plumbing, electric and heating are intricate little processes, and they all have to work in harmony. If your construction plans were followed to a "T" by the subs (the smart ones won't do that), now you've got seven items that fail the inspection (the subs who followed the plans laughed when they installed shit the wrong way). But when Inspector Uberbuilder comes back, he'll find seven more things. (please see "add three months") At some point in your career, you'll pass and get to sheetrock.

Drywall: A perfect compliment to Utah weather. Drier than a dust fart, and dustier than a dirt storm. Something will go wrong at this stage of the game too. Tack on some days, tack on some dollars, and stay the hell away from the job until drywall's done.

Finish: OK smart guy. When drywall is done, your job could be right around 90 percent complete. Many people at this stage in the game say, "Wow! I'm just barely over my budget!" Yup. And this is the fuckin' wakeup call. For some reason of construction psychosis, people don't like anything originally slated for finishes.

Linoleum in the bathrooms?

"You know, I think I'd rather have tile. Ya, Italian tile…with colored grout."

New appliances?

"I like that stainless refrigerator, oh and the Bosch dishwasher, and eew! that Viking gas range…"

Paint?

"Plaster with integral color is pretty cool looking."

This goes on and on and on. 10 thousand forks in the road. Roofing, carpet upgrades, hardwood floors, trim details, stone veneer…lighting! There are actually guys in Salt Lake who get $150 an hour to tell you what kind of lights to get and where to put them. This is the kind of shit that will drive you absolutely mad! You're spending so much money on cool shit that you don't even realize you're still spending money on the unforeseen. Money spentus, tempus wasted, sobriety no longer an option.

C.O.: This means Certificate of Occupancy, and really certifies that you've lost your mind—and all your money. You get to move in, but I've heard of plenty of people so pissed off at this point that they just sell the damn thing.

A few tips:

Cuss: Fucking swear. It's the only accepted form of communication, and it's free therapy. The guys will dig it.

Do some labor: Guys will work harder if you don't look like a Sunday Mormon. At least, sweep up. Never show up in dress clothes.

Beer: At 4:30 p.m. on Fridays, take them beer. Just do it.

And remember: Finalize your budget (with a General Allowance), then stash 30 percent more somewhere else; figure for three extra months. You can't get hurt.

46

Three Rhinolith

The Entrepreneur picks his nose in public. He drills in deliberate motions while working the bugs out of his new plan. This mental excavation many times leaves him looking careless and "eccentric," as he is quite often caught with his pointer finger probing.

The Entrepreneur has figured out all the business games through mining a thousand tough boogers. He can play the "Corporate Good Old Boys" game as well as "Lookin' out for number one." His techniques for business are volatile, but he really knows how to dig out of a paperwork mess; and when things get sticky, he'll always be there to pull the boys out of the hole.

The Entrepreneur would rather see the Boss Man pick his nose than to get caught in a meeting with him, staring at his visible, unknown booger.

The Business Developer prefers to pick his nose on the drive home after a long day. He sings loud with the radio, and thinks no one can see him slowly working with a highly trained touch in the privacy of his luxury car. This is his time.

From his big corner office with two windows, he has drawn out the best associates for promotion, and carefully extracted the day's problems from the company. He feels bad for pointing a finger at a single, stubborn obstacle, but the song's real loud and the windows are tinted, and he'll soon be home—able to breathe free from another dry day.

The Business Developer takes a stab in the elevator once in a while, but he knows it's risky. He also mandated that all employees wash their hands for 15 seconds after bathroom use. He has a clear conscience about that, too.

The Beta Bureaucrat sits nervously in his cubicle and takes an occasional rim scratch. He wouldn't want to get caught pickin' it, or worse yet, get caught screwing around. His favorite phalange works like an apprehensive humming-bird—in and out in a twitching flash—a technique his mother taught him.

On his little breaks, he looks up into the corporate machine and thinks it's much too complicated for him to grasp. He may explore its vast mechanisms, and stroke its lengths, but he'll always move with the heard, stifle a thought, stay solemn in appearance—and should the boss-man start coming, his way,

"Mm-hmm, yup; I'm doin' something—mm-hmm."

A Real Dick

When someone calls a guy a 'worm,' the phallic metaphor is present even if you have to dig for it. A worm is the kind of guy that cuts in line.

Dork is a pretty teen-age insult. A real dick isn't bothered much being called a dork. A dork is the kid that tells the teacher you didn't actually go to the bathroom.

Weenie is the first rung on the phallic name scale with no mistake of meaning. A weenie is a driver who makes a right hand turn with his left blinker on. For that matter, Schnitzel comes to mind.

The beauty of schmok is most people don't even know what it means. "Ha, ha, funny joke, Schmok!"

When Alex Trebek corrects someone's French pronunciation on Jeopardy, Dink is the best word to describe that guy. (I got in a lot of trouble in seventh grade for calling the teacher a dink)

You really only hear meat in the athletic worlds. Meat can be the other baseball team's pitcher, or an endearing name for a well-hung teammate.

To use knob, you have to be pretty cool. It stands to reason; how can you get knob to come off smoothly if you are one?

Personally, I'll only call a guy a unit behind his back. If I'm in good company and I don't want to embarrass everyone with something too offensive, I might chime off something like, "that Fabio's a real unit."

Putz is another to confuse someone with denotation; but trust me, snake's a dick in any language.

And here again, you gotta be pretty cool to call someone a sausage, a tool, or a chode. Any could be used for the guy that just can't say something worth a shit…like Gene Shallot— he's a real chode.

Penis. You heard me.

Penis is the base of it all. You call a guy a penis; you're not messing around with semantics or understatement. You're telling him strait up that his actions remind you of a flaccid network of tissues with no use other than dribbling on a pair of shoes.

Although from penis, you could imagine that calling someone a boner would be a great compliment—but no, uh-uh. A boner is the guy who backs into your car, or George W. Bush when he interrupts The West Wing.

Dick is pretty direct. Dick gets the job done. Dick's casual, but works especially well if it's your boss's name. "Morning Dick!" "What's up, Dick!" "You seem a little harried, Dick!" "Your broker said you're stock's hangin' at four and a half, Dick!"

Bitte and Verga lend an offshore, international insult. They're both in the same offensive bracket as penis, but offer an eloquence that works well when some pompous jackoff demands to dance with your wife.

Pecker may be more bark than bite. It sounds mean with

three hard consonants, but I just can't see Clinton declaring war to Saddam with, "hey Pecker!"

Fuckstick has just enough hard consonants to tell a guy that you're about to take a swing. "Step back, Fuckstick!" is many times followed by a quick tag to the forehead.

Cock is the second most mean-spirited and offensive phallic synonym. Cock is your bastard neighbor when you catch him kicking your dog. Cock comes to mind when your father says the meanest thing he can think of. A cock is a guy who gets a girl pregnant and hits the road.

Prick is reserved for business. Your screaming, bigoted boss is a prick. A client who blows a million-dollar contract is a prick. Five minutes of physical damage would never do justice to a prick. He must be corporately defaced, personally attacked and financially rammed. Information leak; lawsuit; computer generated photos of him having sex with farm animals. A prick must pay the price.

Billy in the Bathtub

(Monologue setup: Bill Clinton is sitting in the White House bathtub, mumbling to himself with an Arkansas cowboy hat on. A 24" Grafix bong sits outside the tub with a half-smoked bowl of extremely potent gift-marijuana from Mexican President Zedillo)

* to be read in the croaky, southern-drawled voice of Bill Clinton *

"Ya, this soak feels good. Now all I need is that little Tanya Harding in here to sit on my lap and make rubber ducky noises. Huh-huh, ya, that'd be nice.

What'a ya think of that soldier? That'd make you happy, huh? All this talk about Reagan's mug carved into Mount Rushmore. If they wanted the real deal, they'd carve out my penis—large and live...ya, that'd be nice. Sure as hell wouldn't wanta' do Bob Dole's dick, all limp and dysfunctional. If they did, it would have to be like a big fat, flaccid joke. It would have to wear a giant blue bonnet that says Pfizer. Ya, there's our forefathers and Bob Dole's foreskin. Ya, that'd be funny."

(reaches for bong, seals the mouth over his lips and tugs)
blib lib lib lib lib, pffffffffftt—cuh; pft; hmpt-hmpt

"Curves. Curves are the best. A woman is all about curves. Hip... butt. I'd like to be friends with all three of those girls on 'Friends.'

The rounder the curve, the more my little guy gets happy. That 'Friends' show is dangerous. That's the whole damn reason I started pluggin' Monika. Saw those curved breasts on TV, glowing in that TV lighting, and those tight shirts, and they always, ALWAYS have hard nipples. Those breasts are round, round curves, and then the nipple, man that thing is the shortest, tightest, sweetest, roundest curve yet. That episode when Jennifer Anniston went out to dinner in that teddy—next thing I knew Monika was in the oval office wanting some petty decision; ya, I remember her nipples... Ya, those were nice. She's a little chubby, but all the best ones in Arkansas were too. Fat bottom girls, you make the rockin' world go 'round. Huh-huh.

I gotta say, Monika drops 40 pounds, and she's got herself a cash-cow future in porn. After I did her, there's gotta be 20 million people that would pay to watch her make rubber ducky noises. Ya.

And if Hillary moves to New York to be a junior senator—then I'll really get strange. Ya, I better start plannin' to blow some shit up. That President Zedillo better keep these buds comin'. And none of that Mexican ditch weed, or I'll show him the biggest lighter he's ever seen..."

The George Dubya Bush "God Help Us All," Global Drinking Game

Bush is spanning the globe, confusing everyone with his no-shit Sherlock philosophies and Dubya dipshitisms. Wild Utah has devised a little game to help us all make it through the next four years.

A popular saying in Colorado is, "Sweet liquor eases the pain." So when Bush gets on TV to ramble and improvise, follow these directions to avoid discomfort or any violent thoughts.

Pick one person to be the MoronMaster. This person will be the final judge for any discrepancies or missed drinking opportunities. Anyone may suggest to drink, but the MoronMaster will officiate over all suggestions.

The Rules:

Drink if George W. Bush does any of the following:

-says any made-up word, especially the words "non-sensical," "common-sensical," or "verbosity"
-gives a thumbs up for any reason
-says the syllables "dub-ya"
-mumbles anything contradictory like, "it's time for the human race to enter the solar system"
-says something painfully obvious like, "for NASA, space is still a high priority"
-includes the word "opportunity" in any sentence
-uses the word "I" when it should be "we"

Chug if George W. Bush does any of the following:

-says the word "abortion," in reference to anything
-makes any reference to (even seemingly) personal agendas
-says anything at all about the economy
-utters the words "The President," whether referring to himself or anyone else

Throughout the game, please keep this in mind:
"Come the millennium, month 12, in the home of greatest power, the village idiot will come forth to be acclaimed the leader." -Nostradamus 1555

Smoke up Jonny (in dual entry accounting form)

Smoking sucks—everybody pick on smoking. It's a heinous act. It stinks. It pollutes the environment. And it's a killer (debit: Smoking Pride, credit: Global Cause).

This sick, disgusting ritual of smoking cannot be explained—except that Big Tobacco markets these foul cancer sticks to children; then on top of it, they put extra horrific shit into cigarettes to make them powerfully addictive (debit: Any Youth's Allowance, credit: Corporate Crime).

Why do people smoke! Tell me! Give me the truth, I can handle it!

(open new account: Simple Fleeting Pleasure)

The sight and smell of fresh cigarettes massages the mind of he who knows their gift. Seeing the embered tip of a lighted smoke across a room is a beacon to the nicotine soothe. Being close enough to hear the feint crackle of someone's first drag is a mind-tingling reminder of what you should be doing. (debit: One Smoke From The Pack; credit: Oh Ya Baby, Here It Comes!)

I'll tell ya why people smoke. The buzz. Smokers love the buzz enough that they're willing to let it kill them. I remember my first drag. I was 22, and lucky for me, someone else was driving my car. I felt like Alice in Wonderland. We stopped to ask directions, but I couldn't even talk. Since then, I've always felt that the legality of smoking while driving is highly questionable. But I enjoy doing it. (debit: My Last Cigarette; credit: Bloody Stinking Denial)

Ponder this for a moment, Mr. Non-smoker. You go out and buy a pint of whiskey to take to a party. Do you share it? Would you give up as much as half to complete strangers? Smokers are the most generous people on the planet. Countless millions of times, a smoker has walked right up to a smoking stranger, asked to bum one, and the stranger will happily remit without any hassle. Come to think of it, marijuana smokers will do the same. So if the notion of charity seems devoid and forever gone from humanity, try bumming a smoke sometime (credit: Nobility Of The Smoker; debit: Grabbin' At Anything Here).

Bummin' a choke is an interesting side note. All cigarettes are not created equal. If you're a Marlboro Man, and the smoke you bum is a Kool, chances are you'll probably look for someone else to bum one off immediately. Then again, if you're a Benson & Hedges kinda' smoker, you might take someone up on a Winston; but four puffs later, you're stubbin' that thing out and verbally punishing yourself for making such a gigantic mistake. I don't know how Drum rollers make it through a day. Frankly, I don't get any kind of buzz—Drums just make me feel putrid. A Nat Sherman on the other hand soaks me on the first draw. I'm forced to extinguish it right away so that I don't land on my face. I'm not really a smoker, but the new Camel Turkish Golds are certainly lovely (credit: God I Hope My Mom Never Reads This, debit: More Than Seven Minutes From My Life).

There are lots of things to smoke out there. I like all of them. Smoking a twice-packed pipe full of fine tobacco makes me feel distinguished. Puffin' on a big ole' dog turd, like a Macanudo or a Playboy Don Diego, makes me feel like my shipment of contraband leaving Cartegena will need to be watched closely. When in Rome, I also like to chew; but I won't go into that disgusting habit too much (it's a wife thing). (credit: Everything In Moderation; debit: Will Make You Die A Lot Quicker)

Some smokers out there can barely hang on without a smoke every four minutes. Some people call themselves smokers, but forget to smoke for up to a week. I for one have never figured out why people smack their pack; cigarettes smoke just fine without it. Zippo's are the way to go. And if you don't think it's lit, just puff it a few times.

I'd like to vie a bowel, please

Of course, anyone with exposure to "the Queen's English" would know the Loo to be the John. And though the British might exude pomp and pageantry, they also have to stop off to the Loo to "pick a daisy" once in a while.

We try to do these things discretely. Exiting subtly, or unnoticed. Using the most distant toilet at someone else's house. Spraying a little mask of flowers—so that it smells like someone shit in the rose garden. But there are times when nature's call is so abominable and barbaric that it can easily become socially acceptable discussion.

The vacuum-type terlets on a sailboat rank among the worst. There is no discretion. There is only the shame that grows until the outbreak of laughter.

After you've finished "posting your letter," you pull the British baton from its clip on the wall, insert it into the pump boot, and then slowly and gently pump and pump and pump. Meanwhile, this guttural slurping noise is moaning throughout the hull, letting EVERYONE know that you're trying to make the bad man go away. Pump, pump, pump. Five minutes of the most tedious and embarrassing exercise a landlubber can do—and then no matter how much you pump, and no matter how hard you try, you can never be certain that it all went down. Add to that the fact of not being able to open the suction-tight lid for 15 minutes, and the process of pinching a loaf can easily take an hour.

Two days of this agony and my wife stopped pooping. The Loo had become a lunch topic, a tea topic, and a paranoiac fascination. After three days, the captain gave us his own poetic instruction on paper. It read:

IMPORTANT!!
INSTRUCTIONS FOR USE OF TOILET

BEFORE USE CHECK THERE IS AT LEAST 2 INCHES OF WATER IN BOWL. IF NOT FILL WITH SHOWER.

ONLY USE MINIMUM PAPER. PAPER IS MOST COMMON CAUSE OF BLOCKAGES. NEVER PUT IN ANYTHING ELSE.

AFTER USE, LOWER LID (THIS TOILET WORKS ON A VACUUM SYSTEM).

INSERT HANDLE INTO PUMP. LEVER UP AND DOWN USING FULL STROKES OF THE HANDLE, SLOWLY AND GENTLY AT LEAST TEN TIME FOR LIQUIDS AND TWENTY TIMES FOR SOLIDS.

NEVER USE FORCE. IF FOR ANY REASON PUMP DOES NOT WORK, CALL THE CAPTAIN FOR ADVICE.

Well isn't that generous? Under the most critical malfunction of his equipment, our trustworthy captain has only advice to offer. (This is without going into impressed review of his beautifully euphonic prose)

As a comfort for this constant reminder of our humanity, I offered this parallel:

On riverfloats through canyons in the West, you're out of contact with anything for days. The laws stipulate, "pack it in, pack it out." There are no receptacles, waste bins or dump zones. So the Loo goes too.

The low man on the totem pole is the bucket boy. He is relieved of almost all other duties but to tend to the terlet.

The rafts stop for the night. The bucket boy finds a secluded spot and sets up. A bush for a screen; an easy place to reach the toilet paper.

Five or more people may take a George, drop the kids off at the pool, or have an Irish Shave. Then the bucket boy gets to apply the enzymes, seal it back up and carry it back to the raft.

This is the truest form of humanity. One is very humbled when he has to carry around everyone else's carrion.

So the next time you're embarrassed about defecating at someone else's house, just remember:

They'd rather have it in the Loo than on their kitchen floor.

Hell: A Unified Theory

OK, we're gonna talk about Hell. In order to do that, we need to make a basis for the discussion. That relies directly on reader religion.

Mormons don't believe in Hell. The Mormon version of Hell is reserved for those who have known the "True word of God," and renounced it. JackMo's (or whatever you call people like this) go to a place called Perdition. There's no fire and burning. In fact, it's very cold, absolutely dark, and very lifeless.

The Christian semblance of Hell is the quintessential Hell. It is almost diametrically opposite of Mormon Perdition. Here, the souls of sinners are sent south to eternally burn for committing acts on earth deemed inappropriate by God. By Christian methodology, the Mormon practice of polygamy gets an automatic, one-way ticket to Hell.

And just to further exemplify the subjective nature of Hell's design, let's consider the Buddhist approach. In the "Vimalakirti Sutra 8" (a book of Buddhist teachings), Hell is put into these terms:

'If there is such a place as Hell, we enlightened beings should certainly go there because that is where they need the help. In order to save people, we volunteer to descend into all the hells that are attached to all the infinite worlds.'

Hell sounds more like a soup kitchen in this instance. Hot enough to make you sweat, but real people have real needs there.

Given that Hell is seen so differently through eyes of varying religions, I offer my own vision. Please, think of this only as patent balderdash—as a Mormon would Christian Hell, and as a Christian would Mormon Perdition. (I openly discern Mormonism from Christianity with no apology to anyone. There are many Christians—but none who become gods)

Being raised part Catholic and part Protestant, and then converting by choice to Buddhism, I have inherent cultural biases that direct my vision of Hell toward the Christian construct. But I ask myself, "Why is it that a pious Christian makes it into heaven for an eternity of pious existence, but a somewhat sinning Christian, who may be a good person but didn't fulfill some requirement, goes to Hell for eternal damnation?" I mean, you're good here, so you get to go be good there. But if you're bad here, you go there to burn, burn, burn. Doesn't seem very balanced.

So because I'm a Buddhist with a Christian upbringing, I'm led to believe that a pious life on earth will reciprocate a pious eternity. And a "sinning" life gets you a like eternity. I don't actually believe in heaven or Hell; it's my story, you're readin' it. (By the way, 11 million Mormons worldwide may envision Hell as Perdition, but our planet is home to almost half a billion Buddhists like me. Hell, South Korea has 11 million Buddhists all by itself!)

So let's say I die, but I'm enlightened. I've "killed the Buddha," which is what the Buddhist teachers taught me to do. There is a Hell, and that's where I'm going—to help people.

I'm in the lotus position.

Being an enlightened Buddha, my eyes are dimly open, and I smile at the beauty of the absolute. My body slips beneath the topsoil, down through a mile of Utah aquifers and breccia, and continues until I can faintly hear the distant tapping beat of Hell.

As I finally come through the last layer of molten earth, I think, 'I have arrived.' The music is surprisingly loud. AC/DC is onstage growling out the Back in Black tune, "Have a drink on me." I laugh when I hear the line, "so don't worry about tomorrow, take it today; forget about the tip, we'll get Hell to pay!"

As I look around, I'm shocked at the scenery. Hell looks amazingly like Cancun during Spring Break. Paganism abounds as beer-drinking frat-boy types are soaked in keggersplash, and topless bikini-girls are dancing everywhere. Not exactly what I expected, but it seems so much more likely than flames and torture.

The acts are vigorous, but not exceptionally vulgar. A "Modern Maturity" type couple is tucked under a cabana, voraciously sucking face. It's the kind of thing a very conservative person might take offense to, however, there seem to be few conservatives around here, and this guy is really taking his time in the pickle between first and second base. Looks like Viagra could be readily available without a prescription.

I stroll over and order a drink. Make it a pitcher...of martinis. Oh my hell, I have people to help. I notice that lounging to my right are Hugh Hefner, David Koresh and JFK. They're talking about Madonna, and sharing a bowl of some incredibly potent smelling KGB...the kind of rope the guys from Amtrak smoke.

I eavesdrop for a minute, and suddenly it dawns on me that there is nothing particularly artistic about Hell. It's a wild party, but its nature is considerably pedestrian. Maybe they do need my help.

The pool hosts an exhilarating game of water volleyball, played exclusively by nude TV news anchors. Now I'm wondering if there is a heaven. As a very wet and well-endowed Walter Kronkite leaps up to spike the ball, he catches himself in the net. He backflops onto the surface of the water, tearing the net away from its posts. As he quickly reaches to untangle his assets, two gorgeous, female news-anchors rush to his aid. They shake their heads, tell him that this ruse is way overused, and that this would (again) be the last time they help him.

Suddenly, a bullhorn appears in my hand. I begin to raise it toward my mouth as if my body was on autopilot. An anxiety rushes over me as I have no idea what to say. These people are partying; who am I to get in the way of that? And I haven't finished my martinis yet.

As the microphone reaches my mouth, my finger pulls the trigger. I think to myself 'well, this will be interesting.'

"You damned people listen up. I've come to Hell to help you."

Immediately, alcoholic fruit is fastballed at me from every angle. What have I done? I pissed off Hell! Everyone is laughing hard. Two former Dali Lamas load liquored melons into a massive slingshot and a third mans the pull to open fire.

Then in the blink of an eye, I'm a grasshopper in a giant field of corn. My whole life, I thought that if reincarnation was the way things really happened, I'd certainly become a grasshopper.

Virtual Humor

by Kevin Duffy

Hell's new marketing strategy:
"The Fat Jolly Satan"

They're Only Whim'in

The saying used to go, "Behind every great man is a great woman." Then through years of sexual revolution and its politically correct reception, the saying changed to, "Beside every great man is a great woman." But I see it differently. I think there's a great woman behind every great man—but she's back there with a whip.

You may raise an eyebrow when I tell you that women's brains are more highly evolved than men's are. It's not only easily recognized, it's scientifically supported. On average, women's brains are 10 percent smaller, but efficiently house just as many neurons and neural connections. Women have a measurably larger corpus callosum connecting their brains' left half to the right; their cell structures for neural communication permanently double during pregnancy. And while aging, men will typically have a 30% increase in peripheral cerebrospinal fluid—an indicator of brain shrinkage—whereas women will only have a 1% increase.

Think of it like this. Back in the days when the hot new technology was "starting a fire," men were hunter-gatherers. We wore ridiculous little loincloths and scurried around eating anything and everything to see what would kill us. That was our job.

On the other hand, women were responsible for everything else. They raised the children, developed the social fabric of the tribe, and fulfilled, by hand, just about every domestic need—which leads me to believe that the loincloth thing was one of their first practical jokes.

"Kilu, I saw the man-skin you made yesterday. It was so funny! I've seen bigger flaps on a hummingbird."

As our civilization developed, women's roles became broader and deeper. Men went from hunting and gathering to punching the time clock. Women advanced intellectually far beyond men and were able to take on more and more duties. By the time Coco Chanel came around, just keeping up with fashion would have been a full time job for men. But women took that on peripheral to hundreds of other tasks. (Want the litmus test? Ask yourself, "Do black shoes look OK with navy blue pants?" If you answered "sure," you were not only talking to yourself, but you have no idea that a parallel universe exists around you) Women are making seventy percent of what men make, but they're running the show.

Anyway, men kept bringin' home the bacon dressed in butt-hair and body odor, and because they felt like they were providing "all the basic needs," men elevated their pig-headed arrogance to the point of never considering that women might exceed them on a cognitive scale.

Now I'll really let the cat out of the bag. (Guys, buckle your seatbelts, because it's much worse than you think) While studying communication in college, I started recognizing the power women possess. Women communicate on verbal, non-verbal and "other" levels that men have yet to understand.

After silently observing for years, I've figured out women's secret. You can call it "Victoria's Secret," or "Secret Antiperspirant," or the "Dirty Little Secret," but I know what it is. Women are telepathic.

I've figured out that when you take 11-year-old girls into a private room to talk about "our changing bodies," you start weaning them from the limited verbal communication used by men, and start teaching them how to read minds, transfer thoughts and manipulate men with the power of suggestion. I'm on to you, and you're going to have to rub me out to keep me from spreading it.

I theorized about it for many years. Then I was at a party with my girlfriend Kat (who's now my wife ((and the origin of that is becoming ever more clear))). I said to my friend Frits, "Hey, let's go listen to Back in Black."

Kat immediately piped up,

"Oh, just go smoke." She was on to us. I quickly back-peddled.

"No Honey, Back in Black is a song by AC-DC." She knew.

"I don't care if you smoke, I just don't want to smell it."

So there it is. I know that you know, and now I'm gonna let everybody know. All I can say is Estrogen is my friend. It evens the playing field just enough to keep it fair. Without it, men would be wearing leather masks and pulling women around in little Fem-chariots.

As they say, behind every man...

The Buzz

LaVerkin, Utah just declared itself a "U.N.-Free Zone." Where do 2500 sheep-shagging, Utah desert rats get off ostracizing themselves from the most delicately balanced political relationship on Planet Earth? We saw the Channel Two news segment on this; the "interview" included a young motherly-type saying, "when anyone spoke God's name, you could hear the thunder outside..." Somehow, LaVerkin claims the Southern Utah Wilderness Alliance has connections to the UN, and that they're trying to tell them how they can develop their land. Ya...um, OK. Didn't your mother ever tell you, "If you keep LaVerkin, you could go blind?"

Rod Decker (speaking of Channel Two) is one of KUTV's 10 o'clock news guys. You gotta check this dude out. He makes news fun, in a Rodney Dangerfield sort of way. One night, KUTV ran a story about the federal government's consideration of making hemp products illegal. Rod covered the story with zeal. He said, 'The FDA believes hemp products still have the intoxicant THC in them; so if I take this hemp lip balm and rub it allll over my lips (does so vigorously), the FDA says it releases THC into my bloodstream.' Oh if it were only that easy, Rod...

In Virgin, Utah, the head of the household is required by law to own a gun.

Former Zions Bank CFO Dale Gibbons is really taking a tough rap. We feel for the guy. He had it all: money, party invitations, intoxicants... Then his daughter got a hold of some drugs, and the next thing you hear is HE'S THE DEVIL! We loved the news coverage on this one. Newscasters said Gibbons was leading a double life. Their evidence: they went into his wardrobe and found on one side, suits and ties—and on the other side, jeans and nice shirts. Whoa! What could be next? Red wine with fish? White pants in October? Look out everybody—he might do something crazy!!

Teen-ager Derrick Sundquist admitted to having consensual oral sex with a 16-year-old girl last year—and became the first Utah man in several decades to be charged with sodomy. Utah law forbids "any sexual act with an [unmarried] person . . . involving the genitals of one person and the mouth or anus of another person, regardless of the sex of either participant." Sodomy was illegal for married people in Utah until 1977. So if you want to take an "alternate route," here's the skinny—Colorado: legal. Wyoming: legal. Idaho: crime against nature, five years to life. Nevada: legal. Arizona: crime against nature (anal intercourse), 30 days/$500. New Mexico: legal. You should also know that intercourse between consenting, unmarried people is still illegal in Utah. But if you're married to her, she can legally consent to your hairy, smelly ass as young as 14 years old. (Pennsylvania, Maine and Iowa are the only other places you can Bring'em Young as 14)

Wildfire Sagehen — If you've ever seen a sagehen, you know what they're all about. You're slowly walking through the wilderness, enjoying the pleasant serenity of it all, and BUDADADADA! Six crazy chickens fly out from under your feet, scaring the living shit out of you. It takes everything they've got to fly 40 feet, then land. Perhaps it's just a rural myth, but it's said that a wildfire fighter with a good arm can drop a sagehen with one rock. Once the bird is wrapped in foil with some wild onions, it can be cooked perfectly in the hot embers of the dying wildfire. It's probably just rumor.

Laughing at the ABC Commission?

A public hearing was held last week for anyone with an interest in Utah's alcohol laws. OK, so you didn't make it. Did you hear about it? Didn't think so. We heard about it, but not in time to get on the agenda. Something smells like shit here, folks.

The ABC Commission hosted a public hearing at the Nazi-architecture, brick building on 900 west. The heading on the agenda read "UTAH DEPARTMENT OF ALCOHOLIC BEVERAGE CONTROL." (These buttwipes complain that the Department has nothing to do with lawmaking or the Commission, but the word "Department" gets used on everything)

The ABC Commissioners were looking much the way we figured they would look on a Friday morning: Vickie McCall (we like her) was dressed in a vibrant green outfit, looking very bright-eyed and bushy-tailed as if she had just consumed a large, fresh cup of coffee. The other four commissioners, bald, beady-eyed and obese, looked as though the notion of falling asleep might be a forthcoming remedy to the indigestion of eleven chocolate-chocolate donuts washed down with two pints of chocolate whole-milk.

We arrived a couple minutes late, so we missed MADD's three representative hat trick. We did get to hear Dave Holliday, representative for the Distilled Spirits Council of the United States (DISCUS). Mr. Holliday was one of the good guys, and very put together; he made it clear that DISCUS has been working in cooperation with MADD for a long time, and that liquor advertising has been restricted from underage markets since the 1930's. This, we hope, made a mark.

Next to speak was Jerry Fenn, an attorney representing the Church of Jesus Christ of Latter-day Saints. You can well imagine the stupid, religious-crusade horseshit Fenn was there to expel. Alcohol consumption this; foolish statistic that... His words and his tone were like a triple dose of Valium, and they just wouldn't end. Fenn droned on as only a hired beta-sub-humanoid can; then, just as we were about to call Dr. Kevorkian, credit card in hand, it ended.

Now, because you missed the meeting, we'll give it to you straight. Adam Ward, Editor in Chief of the University of Utah's Daily Utah Chronicle, gave the next address. This was a pivotal presentation, and rightly so considering college students are at the cusp of legal drinking age. Adam was very composed when he rhetorically questioned the laws mandating alcohol censorship in school publications. He told the commission that the University of Utah administration did their own study of readership, and that when the students, faculty and staff were all considered, only 15 percent or less of the Chronicle's readership are Kool-Aid kids (underage). The fat, beady-eyed male commissioners got their back hair up over this one (eeeooo—gnarly visual, sorry). They grilled

Adam with all sorts of questions trying to discredit the study, then said they would need to see a copy of it.

This was the point in the "public hearing" where it became obvious that the commission was not there to rationally listen to citizen rationale. If someone got up to endorse Utah's 21st century Prohibition in the eyes of God, the commissioners made no comment—but almost nodded as if to bestow powdered sugar blessings on his or her words. If someone got up to question whether these laws are constitutional, economical or even reasonable, the commission was on the defensive as if someone were trying to steal one of the coveted raspberry Bismarck's (except Vickie McCall, who seemed to listen as a reasonable person).

Dr. George Van Komen of the Alcohol Policy Coalition spoke next. He also took the extreme by citing recent European actions and statistics (as if the drunken continent of Europe is even on the same playing field as teetotaling Utah). Get this, when Van Komen was through spewing all kinds of intangible nonsense, the commission asked the good doctor for his help to enforce more stringent laws. Oh ya, that's fucking reasonable guys! Why don't you stick to your Prozac and old-fashioned glazed, and keep your brainwashed little minds out of things like citizens' life, liberty and pursuit of happiness—even if it means they're gonna drink.

We have to say that our favorite part of the ABCC's public hearing was having Melva Sine, President of the Utah Restaurant Association, say, "Let's work together to find meaningful changes to these liquor laws—instead of having you (the ABCC) restricted by a federal court mandate."

Nice work Melva. Way to kick some ass.

64

Patriotic Abstract

First and foremost, I point out that the Constitution of the United States—the very womb from which our rights as Americans were born—specifically provides for the manufacture and sale of intoxicating liquors through the 21st Amendment. In the year 1919, The United States of America tried to prohibit alcoholic beverages; the effort was a complete failure, and the Constitutional Amendment had to be repealed 14 years later.

The 14th Amendment to the Constitution of the United States makes clear that "No State shall make or enforce any law which shall abridge the privileges of citizens of the United States; nor shall any state deprive any person of liberty." By the Constitution, if an American citizen chooses to consume or advertise alcohol, certainly he or she is at liberty and has the privilege to do so.

Most importantly, the 1st Amendment to the Constitution of the United States—the plateau that we have fought over, men have died for, and provides Americans with freedoms beyond all other places in the world—makes two things very, very clear:

1. "Congress shall make no law respecting an establishment of religion." These are the first words of our Bill of Rights. These words mean religion and state are separated. They mean no religion shall make laws, nor shall it try to enforce laws created in vain to control any set of U.S. citizens.

2. "Congress shall make no laws abridging the freedom of speech." This statement is crystal clear, and needs no explanation as to its relevancy to advertising.

Utah State Senator Parley Hellewell is a Mormon. Utah State Representative Roger Barrus is a Mormon. Utah State Senator Dan Eastman is a Mormon who was quoted in the Salt Lake Tribune threatening a personal crusade to limit liquor advertising "whether it's constitutional or not." Senator Eastman is a constitutional sodomizer; obviously he has no respect for the Constitution of the United States—the document that allows him to practice Mormonism and keeps him from the clutches of Terrorism, Socialism and censorship. Senator Eastman, you sir are a disgraceful citizen who takes America's history and hardships for granted.

The sovereign State of Utah clings dearly to a group of 18 "alcohol control states." Utah believes the laws and processes here are akin to all other "control states," and that although "control states" are the minority, they are barely so. I recently spent three days in Michigan—another "alcohol control state." I was off the plane no more than 20 minutes, driving in my rental car, when I heard an ad on the radio for a hangover cure pill. "You wanna have a good time with your friends, right? Just take (brand) before you drink, and no

66

hangover the next day!" Never in Utah.

Two hours up the road, I came to my hometown. The Big Buck restaurant and brewery is clearly visible from the highway—decorated by an outdoor, 47-foot-tall bottle of Big Buck Beer. Certainly Mormon politicians would not let that happen here.

On Sunday morning at approximately 11:30 a.m., my family and I went to Ruby Tuesday for an early lunch. As we sat down, the first words from our waitress were regarding the drink special—Bloody Mary's for $3.25. How could a "control state" allow such a sin?

The next day I drove to Grand Rapids, a staunchly religious city (overwhelmingly Dutch Christian Reformed) in the "control state" of Michigan. Because I was outside the alcohol-lockdown of Utah, I ordered a Long Island Ice Tea with lunch. This cocktail contains one ounce of vodka, one ounce of rum, one ounce of tequila, one ounce of gin (all 80 proof), and one ounce of Triple Sec (a 40 proof liqueur). Drinks in Utah are limited to one metered ounce of hard alcohol. The "family-destroying" cocktail I ordered in Michigan was served hassle-free in another "alcohol Control State."

In brief, the laws and anti-alcohol crusades of Utah politicians are not due to any force other than one single religion—Mormonism. These crusades and laws are doubly unconstitutional: first because they abridge the privileges and liberties of U.S. citizens, and second because they are created by a church. Nowhere else in the United States of America exists a tyranny like this.

—comments submitted to the Utah ABCC by Tommy Kirchhoff, Sept. 21, 2001

The Birdwatcher

Birds he watches with few words.
He walks the country side
in silent stride, looking up in teaks,
in the grasses, glades and palms he peeks,

wishing to touch the gull that's fishing
or slender albatross that glides
and effortlessly rides the rough gales;
to kiss a swift's shoulder as it dives in the dales.

Love the birdwatcher to stroke a dove
on her nape or nose; to rest
his head on robin's breast and find
perverse pleasure in hearing a swan whine.

Flush his ruddy cheeks by thrush's
merry song and excite him without fail
the curlew's feathered tail; he'll lick his lips
rise and quake at sight of swallow's hips

and shake and touch himself by hand
and right away wriggle and sway
when wrens may call he'll like
to grab them all and peppershrike.

One rouge farmer sat and grinned
upon an idling tractor,
his yellow shooting glasses
made fear a vivid factor.
He sat and vibrated
in his favorite field of corn,
while madly chewing jerky,
playing Mozart, reading porn.
Until his twin-lung diesel
coughed within the tractor's snout,
the farmer raised an eyebrow
then the engine's breath went out.
He popped up mired in disbelief,
interrogative in part,
then cursed in French and German
quoting Goethe's "Faust" and Sartre.
That rough rouge farmer turned his head
and fought the angered tears,
as he thought back he winced a smirk,
"tranny's been broke for years…"

Color

from Black
a glimpse of pink to think about
Then Blue and green begin to mingle
into teal
From the moving bluing-Green,
the mixing two yellow to a slightly
orange view
But doubtless to an impatient hue
Rosy Red and embered amber enter on
the scene to push the pastels out
and keep them few and far between
Now shocking pink and electric blue
vibrate to varied hues, to keep
the single silent tone from being too alone
A dash of scarlet and faint of pale
race to join the color scale
while black and white
and those two find
a drying dye
and peace of mind

Rholl

I'll smile when
the colors come
of falling leaves and 'foresnow fun.

All Hallows Eve
of orange and black
shall give me grin of goblin's hack.

I'll pride a pumpkin
of some girth—
a form to feed my macabre mirth.

I'll nod again
put on my porch
and blaze aflame its tiny torch.

For harm to heed
on ghoulish night,
shed shadowed fang and grimsmile light.

With time's tradition's
feet unlashed,
I'll smile too when my pumpkin's smashed.

whenjacks gone

whenjacks gone and we think of that smile,
we'll probably cuss more than once in a while.

whenjacks gone, but his boat is still gassed,
we'll all pull that son-of-a-bitch in too fast.

whenjacks gone, and for sure not around,
we'll guff when we turn his damn TV back down.

whenjacks gone he won't miss it a bit;
we'll get strawberry jelly...without any shit.

whenjacks gone and his bitching is done,
curmudgeons and codgers will sure count less one.

whenjacks gone and this teacher's above,
we'll cry and we'll smile and we'll call it tough love.

12:08   12/08/98

70

Thin

Bearing softly breaches in the balance wearing thin,
my teacup sips a subtle bitter taste—unsweetened sin.
But lack of savored sugar makes not my bitter tea.
A sweetened, social sip alone a thinning balance be.

Tea's a fancy smelling thing to conversation brood—
a delicate delightful thing to set a social mood.
With painted teacup roses, and flowered teapot steam,
the subtleties of sharing truth allow accord—brew deemed.

Steeping barely by the pouch of pekoe without boil,
the liquid strains to smartly gain the glow of amber oil.
But lack of warmth and scant a stir will tea uncivilize.
In solitary mixing thin,
                                        a precious liquid dies.

GOT MILK?

(Pub. SKIING Magazine, February 2000)

While scientists can explain what makes Utah's snow some of the driest in the world, it don't take but a ski bum to predict that Utah will host the world's driest Olympics when the Winter Games come to Salt Lake City in 2002. Utah is infamous for having some of the toughest liquor laws in the country: Shots are metered out in strict, miserly proportions, and most beer available is a watery 3.2 percent alcohol. Which isn't to say you can't get loaded in Utah (Park City, in particular, is chock-full of good bars), but with alcohol-shunning Mormons making up over two thirds of the state's population, the atmosphere is a far cry from that of, say, Garmisch.

And then there's the Alcohol Policy Coalition, a local lobbying group that is pressing for even tougher anti-alcohol laws. Among other things, the group would like to see the under-the-influence blood-alcohol level dropped from .08 percent to .04 percent, heavy restriction placed on Olympic alcohol advertising, and Anheuser-Busch's estimated $50 million sponsorship resold to a less bacchanalaian advertiser.

None of which is likely to happen. According to Utah State Senator Ron Allen, "State legislators see little possibility of changing the current laws." Going even further, some members of Utah's food and beverage industry have expressed hope that the Salt Lake Organizing Committee (SLOC), recognizing that the thirst of a Winter Olympic traveler is greater than that of the average Utahan, would lobby for a temporary easing of Utah's liquor laws during February 2002.

But that is even less likely to happen: "We are going to operate within the existing state laws," says SLOC spokesperson Frank Zang, "and we are making no attempt to change them." Maybe by the time the Olympics get back to Athens in 2004, they'll have changed the Olympic motto to "Citius, Altius, Fortius, Siccus": "Swifter, Higher, Stronger, Sober."

(This is the piece SKIING Magazine published after three or four of my rewrites)

If the Greeks only knew

Whether it's the death sentence by firing line, hordes of polygamists who get the wink from local government, or a "2000-year-old" holy book that coincidentally mimics the words of William Shakespeare, there's only one place where people blame everything on the state—

"That's Utah for ya'."

And while it can be explained scientifically that Utah has the driest snow in the world, it don't take but a ski bum to say Utah will host the world's driest Olympic Games.

The good, money-grubbing folks in Utah have the snow and the mountains to host such an event, but they don't seem to care much for the apres-ski types who attend these things.

Utah liquor laws are some of the stiffest in the country—a far cry from its beer-quaffing cousin, Colorado. This stems from a population that is 70 percent Mormon. There are a few wayward Mormons running around (Jack Mo's as they're known in Utah), but the Church of Jesus Christ of Latter-day Saints strictly discourages the use of caffeine, nicotine and alcohol.

The International Olympic Committee seems to understand the thirst of a Winter Olympic spectator. The committee has been leaning hard on the Salt Lake Organizing Committee to lobby for a three-week easement of Utah's liquor laws. But even if the SLOC were to make some calls, it probably wouldn't get far with the Alcohol Beverage Control Commission. The ABCC is comprised of one normal person, and four anti-alcohol Mormon attorneys. State legislators see little possibility for changes in the current laws.

The top 19 alcohol-consuming countries of the world are all European. The Olympics were born in Greece, which ranks 13th. Maybe by the time the Olympics get back to Athens in 2004, they'll have changed the Olympic motto to "Citius, Altius, Fortius, Siccus." "Swifter, Higher, Stronger, Sober."

(This was the original piece I sent to SKIING Magazine)

Sky

Lying Lingerie

Bras That Don't Need Boobs

At what point did brassieres become less about a little lift, and more about sheer armor? Gazing into my undie drawer, I noticed a horrifying truth. Those cute little comfortable silk numbers were getting shoved to the back corner because of the newer, bigger bra bullies.

These are the bras of a new era. They are large-cupped, under wire versions meant to lift, enlarge and push up the merchandise. What happened to reality? Sometime between Jerry's death (may he rest in peace) and the horrifying outcome of the last presidential election, we ladies were left with little to no options in the lingerie department.

My research (which is completely made up) shows that 80 percent of all bras fall under the "deception underwear" category. There's the wonder bra, the seamless bra, gel bras— shit, I wouldn't be surprised to see sand, water, and syrup bras down the line. Oh wait; they already have the water bra on the market. I forgot.

"It's frustrating for women with breasts, because we don't need all that padding, but there's nothing else out there to buy," says one Park City gal. "It's as if we've seen the magazines and now the stores are assuming that's what we want to look like at any cost."

Ladies, I dare you to look in your undie drawer and tell me you don't have a single brassiere that is a tad, well… padded, in some fashion. Maybe you don't have one if you're a complete hippie chick and can braid your armpit hairs. That's fine. I commend you. But for the rest of us trapped in what retail hell has offered, it's tough to break the habit.

Then there's the male point of view. Let's just call it "The Great Let Down." Ah yes, that's when an innocent Summit County dude discovers the rack on his lady isn't really there at all. It was a mirage brought to him courtesy of Victoria's Big Bad Secret. It can be just as devastating for the girl when he's about to reach over and touch her. She knows what he'll feel, and it won't be her. Instead, it's going to feel like Tupperware tits! Run and hide sweetie.

I say it's time to resurrect those sad, lifeless bras that you haven't looked at in at least a year. Pull them out. Sure, they've been neglected, but it's time to bring them back. Or better yet, go free—there's really no need to lie. If we ban together and refuse to buy what's out there, perhaps we can change the trend. Free your tits! It's natural for them to lay down a bit. They don't have to be perky to the point they're underneath your chin.

OK, that's unrealistic. Most guys love big boobs. If we want to get their attention, perhaps the syrup bra is the first step. Then in the morning, you'll already have something to put on those pancakes.

Springtime Hate

The birds are chirping, that cool springtime aroma is in the air, flowers are set to bloom… and your waitress wants to kill you. Welcome to Park City in April. Yes, we've all had enough. If you're visiting our lovely, cute little ski town this late in the season, there are a few things you should know.

First, we're over it. We've been on our feet serving the public, bending over backwards to please people like you for five months straight, and suddenly, practically overnight, we've lost our shit.

Go to any restaurant to eavesdrop on the workers and you're bound to hear comments like, "Can we just shut down tonight?" or "You can take all the tables… I'll just sit in the closet." Or, "What if we say we all have food poisoning, then we'd have to close."

"Everybody I work with is ready to get out of town," said Beth, a local waitress & hostess & retail clerk (you gotta have at least three jobs here, remember?). "It's like this every year."

Beth and others attribute our lack of patience to several things, the foremost being cheap customers. Bottom line: If you can't afford to go out to eat a meal and tip your server properly, you shouldn't go out. Go to Albertsons if it's out of your budget to pay us what we deserve.

Unofficial, unconfirmed data shows more cheap people come to Park City in the spring than any other time of year. Want proof? Talk to the waiter with the 12-top that ordered one coke, and split 3 entrees. Or what about the group of six that just wanted rice and peanut sauce, and lemon for their waters? I rest my case.

We want to be nice, we really do. And you can help us. Here are a few comments that should NOT come out of your mouth—then maybe, just maybe, we can give you the great service you deserve.

Comments that inspire fuses to blow:
*Oh no thanks, I'll just have water.
*What do you mean there's a gratuity on this?
*We all need separate checks (a 12-person table).
*You were so sweet to us… we'll take good care of you (then leaves a 10-percent tip).
*If we come in at seven, will it be busy?
*I thought you were supposed to have snow.
*Why can't I get a double? You call this a drink?
*Anyone who walks into a restaurant after 9:00 and chooses to camp out for hours may also catch a little attitude.

The Beaver Barber

Not-so-conventional wisdom says it's good to express yourself. Women do this through countless avenues. Dancing, clothing, adventuring, music, sex... the list goes on. One more expressive outlet not to be overlooked: the haircut. There's the trim for your head, and then there's the cut that's good when you're getting head. Yes, the time has come to address how we ladies choose to keep our coif in those ever-popular "nether regions."

TESTIMONIALS

If you've never thought about this, it may be shocking to realize the plethora of options out there for your pubic hairstyle. Take Pam for example; she's now a fan of the Brazilian (to be explained later in this article), but had a Mohawk of sorts some years ago that she dyed bright blue. Yes, her boyfriend was surprised, but pleased at the time and effort she took to be creative and sexy.

One of Pam's pals completely waxes underneath, then goes to the beaver barber and gets a little butterfly pube pattern done up top. Cute, original!

Andrea did the full-on shave-o-rama last month as a "gift" to her boyfriend. The poor guy didn't know what to think and apparently didn't touch her for weeks. *This reaction, incidentally, is a tad odd. Usually the shave is something welcomed by the male species. Advice for girls who want to "go all the way" with their razor... do it with your man as a fun project. The surprise thing can be dangerous, especially if this is not a confirmed fantasy of his.

If you don't shave at all, or even trim your pubes, you may want to rethink that decision. As my friend Mike says, "Women at least need to trim their hair... it will benefit them in the end, because we can reach the goods a lot easier." Ahem, uh, OK. When you put it that way, we get the picture... and like it.

FINDING A BARBER

The biggest challenge for women wanting a good wax for their "downstairs" is finding a quality barber. Usually if you call a salon, you'll find out fast who does them and who does not. Just because that little lady at the beauty salon will wax your brows, doesn't mean she'll deal with you once you've dropped your drawers.

What makes for a good beaver barber? Someone who is fast and efficient, calm and comfortable. When you're having your pubes yanked out by way of hot wax and a tug, there's little room for mistakes or hesitation. If you're on top of the situation, you should visit your barber once a month. It'll cost you about $20. Remember: always tip your epi-stylist.

WAXING IT YOURSELF

Don't, it's dangerous. Chances are good you'll get that hot sticky wax all over. Plus, it's difficult, if not impossible to get a straight line when you're going for it upside down. If you must experience this on your own, just accept the fact that you'll probably burn yourself and end up with an original patchwork design.

THE GROW-OUT

It's a bummer that can't be overlooked: grow-out. It's an awkward and uncomfortable time for everyone involved, but is inevitable once you stop shaving. Oh yes, it will be prickly down there, and could cause minor rashes for you and/or your lover. Advice? Grin and bare it—ha! No really, it should just take a week or two to get through the stubble issue.

STYLE OPTIONS

The Brazilian: this is basically a little stripe of hair running vertically, and centered, or nothing at all.

The Half Little Girl: totally shaved underneath with a tad bit o' fur up top.

Butterfly: waxes down below, beaver barber then waxes in shape of butterfly

Heart: I think you can figure this out.

Barin it all: Ditto

CHANGE WITH THE SEASONS

If this topic is new territory for you, these hot, sweltering summer months may be the perfect time for a new do. Dial up your beaver barber, and say hello to clear cutting.

In The Desert

des-ert\'dez-ert\ n : arid, barren land. A wild uninhabited and uncultivated tract.

With a hot, dry summer just around the corner, it seems appropriate to address the desert. No, this is not a reference to Moab, or even the Mojave. It is simply the best metaphor for those individuals who remain thirsty for sex after a long, long time.

"I am parched, dying, crawling in the desert," my friend Tracey recently told me. After several weeks of "no action," she thought a new young lad would be her oasis. But alas, he was another prick, not even worthy of a pity lay.

"The desert is a lonely place," she explained. "I would just like a little sip of something to keep me going." Some people need hydration more often than others do. The desert is the type of place you can't imagine living in when you're "getting it" on a regular basis. The desert is also a place that seems inescapable once you've been trapped there more than a month or two.

The seriousness of "the dry life" seems to really hit home for women after the four-month marker has come and gone. One local Park City guy says he never worries, even after several months of "no action" has passed. "You've always got Rosie," he said. Rosie who? Oh yea, Rosie Palm, a.k.a. "the hand."

Then there are the few who dare to enter into "The Chosen Desert." My friend Frankie has been on sandy, dry terrain for nearly seven months now. "It's one day at a time," she says. "I'd like to go for a year, because I've never gone that long without it." Fair enough. Temptations are real, and daily for Frankie, "I still get horny as hell." But she insists it's easier to quit screwing people than it is to quit smoking.

In a man's eye, a woman never has to be in the desert. She can step outside her door and get what she needs from any man. But we chicks know it's not that easy. Most women end up in arid lands because of their standards (or so we tell ourselves)— standards we will not lower just to get laid.

Another close friend is about to pass the double-digit marker for months walking on barren plains. "I just figure if nothing happens by this summer, I can take care of this overseas." Yet another justifiable option.

Desert crawling females hear me now! Do not let a mirage take over your good sense. Do not believe that the drunken ski bum you met last night will stick around for any longer than a few hours. Once you face the facts and accept them, you are emotionally free to flee the dry, flat, un-vegetated land you've called home for too long.

Meantime, those of us lucky enough to have landed a lush, hydrated patch of earth; we'll save some water for you. It's nice out here, with the cool breeze, soft blades of grass, and strong, thick trees. Oh yea, we still remember the dry life—and know there will always be visits to the Sahara in the future whether we want them or not.

The Dry Pull

It's practically a fact of life for women who use, well, you know, the plug. You ladies know exactly what I'm talking about. In fact, I can hear you screaming in horror. Men, you're about to learn about one of the least pleasant aspects of menstruating. Actually, I don't know if an explanation is necessary. Let's just say that sometimes we females overcompensate for our "flow." When this occurs, there's only one way out (for the tampon that is): the dry pull.

We know when we've made the mistake—It can be painful, unpleasant, and disgusting. A friend of mine pointed out yet another bummer with the dry pull: "I'm just pissed that I wasted a perfectly good tampon, because I hate to buy them." Good point. I'm a miser too.

I'm not one to advertise in this column, but let me just say that help for these situations has arrived. Thank you Tampax! Yes, the multi-pack is available in stores near you. No longer do you have to commit to using Supers during your entire period... now you can pick your protection depending on how much you're bleeding. Tampax calls the box the "Multi-Pax." Call it what you want, I say it's a damn good, simple, long-overdue idea.

To find out who thought up the "Multi-Pax" I phoned the Tampax Hotline (that's 1-800-523-0014 for those of you with extra time on your hands). Unfortunately, operators were not standing by, so I'll make a grand assumption: A woman finally took charge of marketing at the 'ole Tampax Headquarters and made some changes. I highly doubt a dude would have insight on this one. Still, there are kinks to be worked out with this new product.

For instance, I know women who can't even use Supers.. and want a Multi-Pax with a variety of smaller tampons. Fair enough. It could just be around the corner.

Meantime, this article won't change the world, but just printing the words "dry pull" in a publication gives me some sort of sick satisfaction. Plus, I feel each week we're breaking ground here at Chick Chat to conquer even more taboo babe topics.

The Job That Matters

It's been weeks, perhaps months, since this was first suggested as a Chick Chat topic. Now, after weeks of interviews and grueling research, the blowjob article is coming (no pun intended) to fruition. Relationships of any sort require give and take—therefore, we ladies need to give a little, or more appropriately, a lot when it comes to going down on men. There are women who consider their style of giving head the best, and take pride in it; and there are others who may be a tad sheepish about the act. One thing men and women agree on: desire. Desire is the key ingredient to a fabulous BJ. Here are a few odds and ends regarding blowjobs that may help us all in handling the merchandise properly.

YOU ARE WHAT YOU EAT. Laugh if you will, but what you put in, truly comes out. Pineapple consumed the day before makes a tasty treat for the recipient of your sperm. This tid bit comes to us from Andrea who is a dick aficionado. Stale beer is the flavor she's generally used to. This may sound gross, but she says it's like home, something familiar, and that the flavor is really quite mild.

Blowjobs should be avoided when your man is taking any sort of medication (the taste is similar to when you get an aspirin caught in your throat and don't have enough water to wash it down).

THE TEA BAGS HAVE IT. Unofficial research shows men are lovin' the tea baggin'. They name it their favorite technique for the BJ. This has nothing to do with Lipton.

WATCH THE TEETH. The most common complaint from men who have been unfortunate enough to receive bad oral attention has to do with their partner using her teeth. Bad move. No teeth ladies (duh) just lots o' saliva. One bad nick and the hardon could be history.

EFFORT. Let's face it. Blowjobs can be a lot of work. Tired jaws, tired arms, drool all over the place at times. Most guys appreciate the hell out of a girl who will at least try, and they generally come in 5-10 minutes. Andrea's current boyfriend is a rare exception to the 10-minute rule. She says 25 minutes is about the shortest possible, and 45-60 minutes is the usual, which takes stamina on the girl's part.

ADVICE. A former colleague of mine claims that he can tell by the shape of a girl's eyebrows how adept she will be at giving oral sex. His number one piece of advice is that you have to love the penis beyond all else. He says that a guy can tell if you are licking it because you have to, or if you're doing it because you NEED it and will wither on the vine if you don't get it.

AH YES, THE SWALLOW. Some say it needs to be done—and this is true for some folks…. But I don't know any men who have thrown a woman out for not swallowing, or would utter any complaints if they had a good job. If you are swallowing, it will taste best if you're with a vegetarian (see

"You are what you eat"). Professionals in this arena recommend taking it in fast, right down the hatch so you don't end up with the gook sloshing around in your mouth too long. If you'd like more details, check out Playboy; this has apparently been a hot topic for the past few months with many women writing in, offering their views on the much-talked-about swallow. It seems many women are now reading the publication "for the articles."

THE BLOW THAT BLOWS. Men, be patient. If your lady is a novice, and is at least trying to help you out, enjoy. And, if you're lucky enough to meet someone that loves dick more than life itself—jackpot. Male subjects interviewed for this piece say they'll be patient, just don't deny them. Ladies, your efforts will be rewarded if you're with a good guy— Andrea got a trip to Mexico where she delivered a two-hour blow job, and upon finishing, her lover screamed "hallelujah!" No need to ask if he enjoyed that marathon.

"EXTREMELY BILLY"

…all characters in this article are real, and only some of the names have been changed.

You've met him, dated him, and dumped him. Don't do it again, or you'll get another beener for your birthday.

Some call it a widespread epidemic that's hitting small, mountain towns the hardest. Hundreds of this specific male breed have been overpopulating areas like Aspen, Tahoe, and of course, Park City for years. These men are elusive, they try not to shower, and they sprinkle their limited vocabulary with terms such as: glissade, crevasse, retundo, and dude.

If you've lived here long, you've most likely slept with a few, and maybe even tried to have a relationship with one. Whether his name is Extremely Bryan, Extremely Joe, or Extremely Ryan, he's the same man deep down. He has limited communication skills, which is why he spends the majority of his free time with elements that don't talk well either. Next to rock, ice, water, snow, and dirt, he's a regular conversationalist.

How do you know you're in the sack with "extreme guy?" If one or all of these have happened to you…

*You got a fly fishing vest for Valentine's Day

*You know the back of his ass (from a distance) better than any other part of his body from trying to keep up with him for months…

*Vacations are contests.

*Everything is a contest.

*He doesn't share his orange with you.

*You find yourself at the top of a mountain or bottom of a canyon, where you never wanted to be in the first place, alone, and you know he's not waiting, just congratulating himself on his performance.

*You met each other at one of the following: A Phish concert, in line at REI, Ray's Tavern, the Bit and Spur in Zions, the Mangy Moose in Jackson, Nepal, or in physical therapy.

Men who can do things are great. Men who can do things well are good too. It's the attitude that comes with "Extreme Guy" that no one needs. "Dude, did you see me? I was flat spinning in that hole, and it was so sick…" or "It's all crimpers and slopers and there's no big fat jugs." Blah, blah, blah.

Extreme Guy has usually had a laundry list of injuries: broken collar bone, hyper extended thumbs, blown out knees. Crutches accompany mounds of gear in closets, in the garage, and his bedroom. Nine out of 10 Extreme Guys have a dog, and that dog's name is in some way related to the Grateful Dead. You know, Bertha, Jerry, China Cat, Althea, etc.

Ladies, if you choose to embark on an Extreme Relationship, here are a few tips: 1. never complain 2. never ever compete 3. never care 4. and remember, you'll never be as good as he is; if you get close, you'll get dumped.

Let's keep one thing straight; not every guy who is into outdoor adventures is an Extreme Dick. Quite the contrary. You know who you are. If you have no patience, and not enough generosity to give your gal an orange wedge… well, then, you're sick dude. I mean it.

Dustin Sturges

Back to School

Kayaking. I know what that is. It's a bunch of idiots, stoned out of their gourds, floating down a stretch of white water that was never meant to be run—in what is probably the most unstable boat ever made. OK, I'm surrounded by idiots. I just want to be able to do what they do in a kayak. I'm well aware that there are relatively painless ways of learning how to do just about any outdoor sport.

While I used to laugh at the group of friends who came to town to ski with that one incompetent member, I was the one that got him equipped and set him loose on the slopes to figure it out for himself. I just can't bring myself to take a real kayak lesson. Consequently, I recently found myself injured and quite often wet. Once again I've enrolled in the "Keep-Up" school. The "Keep-Up" school is the most widely franchised school in the country. It's the one where the instructor doesn't waste time going over the unimportant basics of the sport. He just does his thing and tells you to, "Keep up!"

There are "Keep Up" schools in every sport in every town. I have been taking sporadic classes in this school of kayaking for seven years. I'm a slow learner. I took my first class while I was still in high school. At that time, my friends had recently taken up the sport after graduating from the "Idiots on Parade" school of rock climbing with me. One of them had

extra gear, so he put me in the boat, strapped the skirt down (the skirt goes over the cockpit to keep the water out), handed me the paddle, kicked me in the river and yelled, "Lean down stream!"

I yelled back "What!?" and promptly tipped over. I eventually figured out that one has to pull the skirt before one is able to exit the boat. Soon I was happily bobbing down the river, sans boat and paddle, bouncing off whatever rocks came my way. After much ado, I retrieved all my gear and got back in the boat. I swam (abandoned the boat) ten times that day, but ended up coming away from it with just a black eye, and some scrapes and bruises.

I called it quits for a while. I figured floating down a river in a plastic banana with a death grip on my butt (whose natural position is with me under water) was a stupid sport. Unfortunately, I am sometimes not a smart man. I found myself a year later, half drunk, almost in the dark, flailing desperately—trying to roll the boat back up at the put-in of the alpine section of the Snake River. Some time after dark, my instructor ("Lean down stream!") concluded that I was hopeless and gave up.

I showed up back at the put-in the next morning. I was equipped with a full wet suit, dry top, (I still can't figure out why I needed to put a dry top over a wet suit), five layers of fleece, booties and a ski hat under my helmet. The day was a scorcher, but the river was ice cold and I planned on doing a lot of swimming. I ran the entire thing and didn't tip over once. I think I lost ten pounds that day sweating into that wet suit.

Since then, I've run quite a few rivers and gotten pretty stable in the boat, which is good because I still don't have a roll. I've had some roll sessions and can roll in a pool, but once I tip in the river it's all over.

After a recent trip to the Clark's Fork River in Montana, I decided that I probably ought to learn how to roll so I did not die trying to keep up. All of my former instructors are now sponsored by kayak companies that fly them all over the world to shoot movies of them doing incredibly dumb things in their boats. As they run bigger and bigger waters just for a nice relaxing day, keeping up starts to become dangerous. So, I'm back in school. I found a nice little classroom on "The Mighty Weebe" and I'm there quite often.

Should you care to join me, I'll be the guy floating down the river with a boat in one hand, a paddle in the other, and many beers in my pocket. It is conceivable that some day I'll graduate, but probably no time soon.

Cold Beer and Shrinkage

Rachel and I went down to Southern Utah a few weeks ago so that we could get my raft out of storage. We drove all night and got to Durango at about 2 a.m. As the sun came up, we gathered our 30-year-old Udisco raft and hit the road.

We sped North along highway 191 to Moab. We turned in at the Potash road and almost ran off the road a few times looking at the roadside climbs. The dirt road at the end of Potash is well maintained and, after many miles, connects with the White Rim trail that runs the length of Canyonlands Park.

We got to the boat ramp at the put-in for Cataract Canyon just beyond the gigantic hole in the canyon that is the Potash mine, and unloaded. The shuttles were dispatched for the long drive down to Hite Marina where the plane was being readied to fly people back to Moab. For most of the day, we tried our best to get the mountain of gear we brought to fit into the twin Udiscos and the brand new perky NRS boat we had rented. I have no idea how we did it, but we did. The other Udisco had been bought by some family friends when we bought ours; it was captained by the oldest son from that family, O-man.

Adam Olsen got the name O-man from the many occasions that the rest of the tribe would sit in the eddy watching him through the cracks of their fingers unable to say anything but "oh, man!"

For the next four days we rowed. Flat water is an arduous task to undertake in a raft. Your hands get hard, and your back gets sore. Luckily, each night we were treated to the culinary masterpieces that Scott and his girlfriend Alex had brought for us. After dinner we would pass the guitar around the campfire until we fell asleep. Between five musicians we never ran out of songs.

We all awoke rather sluggishly on the fifth day, having had a layover day to patch the Udiscos and lighten the load of beer we had brought. The early morning was spent getting everything strapped on as securely as we could. The law of averages says at least one out of three boats will flip in the rapids we were running that day. Fortunately, we had partied like rock stars the night before, so almost everything heavy went into the NRS boat, leaving the leaky Udiscos well above the water line.

As we rowed out, a chatter of fear-sparked excitement went through the entire group. We had all run white water before, but O-man and I had always been on the business end of the bail buckets that were now faithfully manned by Rachel and John in my boat, and by Steph in O-man's. The sun was beating down and we were all happy at the prospect of getting a little wet—at least as we floated past the Doll House. The Doll House is a twisted, odd formation that looks like something out of a Salvador Dali painting. We listened to what sounded like a 747 airliner flying low up the canyon and enjoyed the calm before the storm.

Coming into the first rapid, I was having doubts about my ability as a boatman, but the four previous days of flat water rowing served me well. The canyon dropped away below us and sucked us in. I turned and twisted the boat to meet each four-foot wave as it came. We got a little bit wet, but the line that our fleet of five kayakers picked was always good.

Cataract Canyon consists of about 20 rapids, but only four are named: Mile-Long (aptly named), and Big Drops One, Two and Three (also aptly named). We read and ran Mile-Long and Big Drop One without stopping, but as the cacophony from down stream began to deafen us, we pulled over to scout. The sight that greeted me, as I topped the rise we had parked behind, could only be described as terrifying.

The river, already running fast, narrowed 30 feet and dropped 20 in the space of a few hundred yards. Jagged, house-sized boulders jutted out of the middle like the teeth of an enormous pre-historic beast waiting to close its jaws on anyone daft or unlucky enough to find themselves in the middle of them. The school-bus-sized holes were the throat of the creature and standing up above them, I was sure I could see clear to China.

We sat there contemplating the true meaning of stupidity as we chose our lines—left of the first tooth then pull right for all that you're worth to avoid the throat, and ride the tail into the eddy at the bottom. Scott was the first to go. We watched as he paddled out into the stream, his kayak looked like a child's paper boat in the raging torrent. He hit the first wave

and disappeared, surfacing 30 feet down the stream upside down. He rolled back up, gave a hoot of triumph, and eddied out.

O-man was next paddling raft A (the Udiscos were labeled A and B in ancient, fading spray paint). He dropped in and headed toward the first tooth. He misjudged the distance and had to paddle forward to avoid the rock, killing his momentum. He missed the rock, but was sucked straight down the throat of the beast. All of us on the shore held our breath as he squared up to the hole, calm as Buddha and grinning like the Cheshire cat. The raft stopped dead as it hit the massive wall of water. It then folded violently in half, right on top of Steph. Just as we were pulling the body bags out of the other rafts, the monster spit out raft "A" with extreme prejudice. After a full mid-air three sixty, O-man was able to straighten out and paddle to the eddy, still calm and grinning. The roar of cheers from up river could almost be heard over the roar of the beast. Two more boats to go.

I was next. Being the least experienced boatman of the group, I wanted to be in the middle of the other two rafts (so the first could show me the line, and the second could pick up the pieces after I screwed it up). I returned to my raft and informed my passengers of our position. "O-man just got schooled. I think we're going to die." Luckily, my boat-mates were much more optimistic than I was, (poor fools) and we shoved off.

"Left of the rock—not too close—pull right—NOW!" The

teeth passed by on the right, and the throat on the left, just as we planned. We got some minor slaps from the tail, but made it to the eddy in good shape.

As my bailers went to work, I concentrated on breathing. Time for the last raft. An experienced boatman named Chad, whom we had also grown up with, was rowing the NRS boat. It was the only one of the three that was guaranteed not to sink on the flat water, so we had loaded it down with everything we could fit into it. Unfortunately this made the boat too heavy to avoid the throat, and in went another. The three thousand-pound raft barreled into the throat. When it hit, it bucked violently, heaving two of the three passengers 10 feet into the air. Then just by sheer merit of mass, it punched through the other side. The passengers soared like eagles and dropped like rocks. They hit the water about 20 feet apart.

Alex swam back to the NRS, and the other (who shall remain nameless) rode the tail into the eddy where he climbed aboard our boat. All I could do was hand him a beer and laugh. He had been in a kayak, swam Mile-Long and Big Drop One, gotten into the raft, and ended up swimming Two anyway.

We scouted Big Drop Three. It looked fairly straight forward; line up 10 feet off of the first tooth, miss the throat of death on the right, and ride it straight out the other end. O-man went first again. "No worries, no hurries, no panic." Unless he gets swallowed, he makes everything look so easy. This one he just danced through.

I was next. I had to get lined up fast because there was a strong current going the wrong way. We followed the eddy line around and pulled into the maelstrom a little too late. I was pulling with everything I had, but it just wasn't enough. We were headed for a large rock, but that wasn't my main concern. I was concerned about the giant hole on the other side. We narrowly missed the rock on the wrong side. Everyone in the boat cheered. "Don't cheer yet! We're screwed!" I screamed, and pulled for our lives. The looks of stark terror on the faces of John and Rachel as the monster hole reared its head just down stream would have been hilarious if I had not been in the same boat. I was rowing as hard as I could, and was amazed to see the hole pass by on the right as I squared the boat. Not exactly as planned, but a good line anyway.

The NRS boat pulled through the last drop without a hitch and we rode the river on to camp. The sun slowly set in the west and the tribesmen all drank for their swimming. One beer out of Woody's river bootie for each incident. Tales of river heroism filled the still canyon darkness.

Fireworks Safety

Here we are again! It's time to celebrate our great nation's independence by getting real drunk and blowing shit up! And since we live in Utah, we get to do it twice!

I think Pioneer Day doesn't really need to be celebrated anymore. Back in the day, the pioneers were celebrating being able to have 10 wives who would shut the hell up when you told them to. That's something to celebrate! Now you can't even have two wives without getting arrested, and even if you do, they'll never shut up when you tell them to.

Be that as it may, any excuse to party is a good one. We here at Wild Utah know that most of you are responsible, but we also know that after that fourth Tequila shot and the hallucinogens that inevitably follow, even the best of us turn into slobbering idiots. When all that good sense goes out the window, it's a good idea to have a solid set of fireworks rules.

1) Find a nice clear area to light your fireworks in. If you can set up somewhere with a clear shot at that damn yappy dog of your neighbors, so much the better.

2) Always make sure that there is plenty of liquid around to extinguish whatever you light on fire while you stagger around like an asshole with that sparkler. We have done a lot of experimentation with this one, and have found that Olympia beer works best—after all "it's the water." Make sure you have at least a case at all times.

3) Make sure your underwear is not acrylic! Synthetic underwear has a tendency to melt to your nuts when you are trying to piss out the lawn fire that got out of hand because you ignored #2.

4) This one is important: Utah fireworks suck! Not only that, they are dangerous! There has been much loss of eyebrow hair because of this stupid ban on all of the fun fireworks. Wyoming is just an hour drive. Don't be lazy! They'll sell anything short of a full stick of dynamite.

5) Avoid confusion: If you are having a bottle rocket war in the back yard, stick to bottle rockets. Roman candles can be very distracting and can destroy your night vision, making that little old lady walking her poodle by your back yard look just like your loony friend—you know, the one who comes to all your barbecues in full combat fatigues.

6) Pretending to have had your eye blown out to get your friends close enough to drop a firecracker down someone's pants is cheating!! If you really want to scorch someone's ass, proper etiquette demands that you run them down on foot, tackle them, and stuff that thing the hard way. It would probably be a good idea to look at #3 one more time.

7) In these times of severe drought, try to avoid roman candle wars. If it looks like roman-armed conflict is inevitable, go inside. Structural fires are much better for roasting marshmallows.

If these seven easy steps are followed, Wild Utah guarantees that your fourth and twenty fourth will be safe and fun!◊

Footnotes: 1. Wild Utah does not guarantee anything of the sort.

2. For the Park City Police department: I do not condone any of the aforementioned appalling behaviors; I have only one wife and Dustin Sturges is just a penname.

The Sturges Chronicles

This story is brought to you by e-mail from Dustin and Rachel Sturges on their travels through Thailand and New Zealand. This was a journal entry from New Zealand, mid-January.

Hello Everyone!
Much sport climbing at Payne's finally led to boredom. One of the two Britts we have been hanging out with for the last few weeks and I decided to climb Cloudy Peak outside of Christchurch. The girls were just going to hang out in town, so Gary and I geared up to do The Great Prow. It's a climb in one of the wilderness areas that goes at Aussi grade 14, and is about 1000 feet of climbing. We left the Ford and got a room in Nelson about half way there.

After the bars, the next morning offered a very unsuccessful trip to the store and an endless drive to the mountains outside Christchurch. The back peaks splayed themselves against the horizon, reflecting the perfect sunlight with quiet majesty. They were very imposing.

We camped that night with the girls next to a lake in a low valley. The next morning, we headed back to the last town we passed to get everything we had forgotten during the hangover-shopping episode in Nelson. This accomplished, we headed down the dirt road to the Ewrahon Station.

The Ewrahon Station is nestled on the side of a convergence of two massive glacial valleys. We were supposed to sign an intention book at the ranch, but when we got to the gate there was a sign that read "God will forgive your trespassing after I shoot you." I crept into the yard with both hands in sight. It turned out not to be as serious as all that though. The young lady who looked after the place met me. She showed us to the book and drew us a little map to get us where we wanted to go (since the guidebook didn't have one). Before we knew it, we were on our way. We hiked down a 4WD road to the glacial valley proper. It was about a mile across before it met with the second valley (also a mile across) that we were going up.

The river that ran through the first valley was the Clyde. It broke up in about 10 little rivulets across the gravel basin. We crossed all of the rivers, none more than knee deep, with the sun on our backs and the wind gently pushing us along. We came to the next valley and followed the Havelock up to what we assumed was the Cloudy Stream. After going about three hundred yards into the smaller valley, it became apparent that there were actually two valleys that the stream came from.

We took the right hand valley, trusting in the girl at the station because the guidebook said the valley should be obvious. We cussed and spit our way about a mile up into a high valley through neck-deep brush and a plant that, I could swear, feeds on human blood. In the middle of each, we were trying the whole way to guess which rock face (out of the three thousand) we were supposed to climb. At about 8 p.m., exhausted and disheartened, we gave up and made camp (sort of). The flattest spot we could find was sort of a small step just below where the scree wall of the canyon went steeply up. We made dinner, drank three liters of wine, and went to sleep (the ground was just rocks). We were awakened at about 4 a.m. by the ceiling of the tent banging on our faces. All of the stakes had been ripped from the ground and the wind had almost succeeded in throwing the tent off of the mountain with over 100 lbs. of gear and two grown men. It continued to blow viciously from all directions, pounding rain through the tent at over 100mph. We could do nothing in the dark, so we waited, cold and wet, until 6 a.m.

I was dreaming of drowning in the Arctic Ocean when I awoke, still surrounded by dark blue (the color of the tent), still freezing, and still almost submerged. The tent was rebuilding itself between gusts, only to come crashing back down again when the next one hit with the force of a freight train. We finally steeled ourselves and packed up inside the tent. Gary had to get out and hold the tent while I threw the packs out and jumped out to help him. We found that everything we had stashed under the fly had flown. My stove, a helmet, my coffee cup and some other stuff were nowhere to be seen.

We quickly packed the tent and started searching the slope, just pausing long enough to note that the tent had moved almost a meter from where we set it up (while we were inside it). The search for our wayward gear was impeded by the gusts of wind blasting rain out of the steep valley like a shotgun, knocking both of us flat every thirty seconds. We found the helmet, one of the pots and my coffee cup 100 yards down the slope. We set them next to the packs and went to look for the rest. We got about five feet away before the next gust knocked us flat. When we had picked ourselves up, we had to find everything again. We settled on one pot and the helmet, counted ourselves lucky and left.

As we staggered and tumbled back down the way we came, the clouds began to let up even though the wind did not. We took a break about 1000 feet from the valley floor. As we lit our smokes, the sun came out and threw a rainbow all the way across the mile-wide valley. It was brilliant, almost blinding. As we extinguished our smokes, an even brighter flash lit the sky and something like a 1000-pound charge went off in the clouds. It was amplified by all of the valleys until it was loud enough to send us running and rolling through the pissing rain as fast as we could to the valley below.

Once we got to the valley floor, we stopped and cooked some coffee over a tuna can filled with ignited methyl alcohol. Slightly warmed, we packed our tuna can and our one pot, and started the long flat march out to the van and the girls who wouldn't be there until tomorrow.

The Sturges Chronicles II

As we met the next huge valley, the clouds dissipated and the wind picked up to around 90mph. All of the semi-clear little streams we had crossed yesterday were raging, whitish-brown rivers. Gary and I locked arms while moving one at a time across several crotch-high, very fast moving streams, trying to get to the far side of the valley.

Finally, after a nearly disastrous crossing, we ended up on an island looking at the last, fastest, and biggest river we had to cross. After a few false starts, we decided there was no way we were going to get to the other side with the waist-deep water moving at 30mph and the wind doing 90 in the same direction. We took a last look at the end of the trail, an eternal 100 meters away, and surveyed our options. Though it wasn't raining on us, it was pissing on the mountains.

While we were thinking, the island we were standing on got smaller and smaller. Gary spotted a hut on the easier side of the river, so we went for that. The problem was that the river had risen six inches while we were deciding, and the stream that had almost drowned us on the way in was deeper and faster.

We leap-frogged out, until almost halfway across the 20-foot-wide stream. We were very unstable and up to our waists in water. Gary was behind me and yelled to go back. It was too late. My feet were already being taken out from under me,

so I let go of his hand; I staggered two more steps toward the far shore, and toppled into the freezing water. My 60-lb. pack did not, as I feared it would, pin me immediately to the bottom; and as the current swept me along, I was able to claw my way to shore.

I dragged myself out of the water and immediately stood up. Gary was on the other side of the river still standing on our diminishing island. I tried to yell something encouraging through my chattering teeth, but all that came out was, "I soaked my damn cigarette!" and something like a maniacal laugh.

Gary, seeing that he had no choice but to cross made two false starts, each time staggering back toward shore. Then, seeing me become hypothermic in the gale force winds, he went for it. He made it almost halfway across before keeling over and swimming/crawling toward shore. No longer being of sound mind or body, I did the only thing I could do; follow him down the river on the shore screaming, "Swim mother fucker, Swim!!!" He followed my advice and beached himself through no small effort.

Saying almost nothing to each other, we set off at a marathon pace for the hut. When we reached the hut, we found it in general disarray. It was a sheep shearing station. I assumed it was on this side of the river because the sheep are smart enough not to be persuaded to cross the damn thing. As it was, the hut was filthy and covered with some kind of chemical powder. The yard was, however, in the sun and sheltered from the wind.

We hung everything we owned on the fence to dry, and made coffee. Everything dried and the weather cleared.

Our current situation is this: The girls are coming to pick us up tomorrow and we are out of food and coffee, and completely sick of being here. If the weather holds, we should be able to cross the river on foot. If not, I am going to try and swim it towing a rope. It can't be more than 50 feet wide, and I'm fairly sure I can do it. I'll be carrying the dry pack with a plastic bag of (hopefully) dry clothes and the inflated wine bag. If I don't make it, I'm sure this will be found once the water drops. Give my wife and my family all of my love. Life has been great and hopefully these last few lines have been unnecessary. Guess we will see.

1/17/01

Last night was one of the longest nights of my life. We were out of wine, so after we packed up we had a cup of coffee and settled in. The sky had begun to cloud over again and we were pretty tense about the morning. I couldn't get any sleep thinking about that huge milky river roaring past me. I spent the night listening for rain.

This morning we awoke to cloudy skies and building wind. We couldn't tell if it had been raining up in the valley, but it looked like it was going to soon. We cooked the last of the coffee over the tuna can and quickly broke camp. By the time we reached the river, the wind had died down a little and we were able to pick our way across the mile-wide water system without a problem. The water had gone down a few feet. When we crossed the very last waterway we were so elated that we walked back into it for a picture.

We are now sitting by the side of the road waiting for Rachel and Sharon. The girl that gave us directions passed by with a herd of sheep and said that she forgot to tell us it was the second big valley. Oh well, we were dumb for not having a map. There's always next time.

Back in the Saddle

Well, back in town actually. It's pretty weird after being away so long. I'm having a great time seeing all of the lunatics that one tends to call friends after too long a period in this town.

I was cordially invited to the Wild Utah employee party. That was a "far from sobering" experience. Rumor has it that one of our flock ended up puking all the way down the canyon (much to his designated driver/girlfriend's chagrin). The Publisher got so drunk that his wife almost went into labor just from the fumes when he finally collapsed into bed. He probably won't let that one out the door, but just in case, videocassettes of the whole shindig are available at beerbath.com, or for $20 at the Wild Utah office.

My articles have always been about what's going on in my life, so let me fill you in. I own a house here, and I've rented it out. I have been on both sides of this agreement now, and let me assure you—you are always better off being the screwer than the screwed.

I have renters straight out of a Stephen King novel. All right they're not that bad; but sitting in New Zealand with an overdrawn bank account and an outstanding camping bill with "Willie the mad camp director" is a learning experience. This is like figuring out that there is an exact position one has to assume to get his zipper up safely—very unpleasant.

For the most part though, I still have to assume that people are basically good. The problem is that some have very convenient lapses in conscience. I don't like to name names or anything, but the pay sucks and if we here at Wild Utah weren't able to exact merciless bloody revenge with a blunt object like the god honest truth, there wouldn't be much point. So let me tell you about my ex-renter.

This bastion of human integrity couldn't just be content to screw his landlord like the other three ex-renters (who shall remain nameless due to my benignant nature). He had to screw me and the poor girl he got to cover his lease. This fine young man made it clear to me, in a house meeting, that he was leaving for Europe, and skipping out on his year lease—but that he was getting a replacement. I (very stupidly) had forgotten to get my phone disconnected before I left, and after making sure whom the phone belonged to, the dip-shit ran up an eight hundred-dollar phone bill on my tab.

I told him I wouldn't press charges if he painted the house, he being a professional painter and all. The house now looks like Jackson Pollack had a monstrous orgasm in the middle of the living room.

This guy is now in Europe, but I didn't get the worst of it. Nooo—the young lady he was getting to move in cut him a check, thinking that he was paying the rent with it until the lease was switched over. He and her money were out on the next flight to Cleveland with a connecting one to Luxembourg.

Hope ole' shit-bag doesn't have to come back through Salt Lake City. He's liable to find plenty of his blue suited friends waiting at the terminal for him. By the time he gets back, there will be plenty of proceedings to keep him occupied. That, however, is none of my business.

I finally found some great people to fill the space that dickhead and his buddies left, and am therefore pondering my own dilemma—the lack of a roof over my own head.

Rather than doing something drastic like getting a place here and a real job, I think my wife and I will go south with a snow shovel tied to the hood of our truck until someone asks us what it is. So begins the next section of our journey together, "On the Road."

Tips for Tolerating Co-Tenants in a VW Bus

Many years ago, in a galaxy far, far away, I lived in a bus on BLM land outside Zion National Park. I didn't exactly live in the bus. I had my own truck. The guy who owned the bus was my climbing partner. The bus was a pop-top and my buddy slept "upstairs;" so the downstairs was the living room. On nights that we weren't climbing, we would congregate there, and drink ourselves into a coma with cheap, boxed wine. Things got a little tense every now and again, but all in all, these were some of the best times of my life.

One would think that this would be a definite step to simplifying one's life—not so. The dynamics of living in close proximity to another human being boggle the mind. As such, and having done this for a while, I have some ground rules that will guarantee at least tolerance if not happiness.

1. IT'S THE LITTLE THINGS THAT COUNT. Any little idiosyncrasies that you have will annoy people; get rid of them or take them outside of the bus. I realize that this is extremely difficult for some people. For a while, two girls were sharing a bus next to ours. One of the pair liked to listen to "Rage Against the Machine" at high decibels. Although she was widely hated throughout the campground, we all had to live with her. One particularly loud session ended with the sound of a little blonde forehead being bounced off of a flimsy, odd-shaped radiator. We never saw either of them again.

2. KEEP YOUR STUFF SEPARATE! There is nothing more conducive to homicide than an argument over who has dibs on the joint-purchase, shit shovel.

3. ALCOHOL AND DRUGS ARE GOOD. Living in a two-story VW, someone is going to step on someone's face when they get up in the morning. This is fact. The more sedated the both of you can be, the better.

4. KEEP ALL OF YOUR STUFF PACKED. You think it's bad having a messy roommate? Try subtracting 1000 square feet from the equation.

5. BE ABLE TO TAKE LONG WALKS. Preferably these walks should last a few days. There is no better thing for a plutonic relationship than time off (if you do not own the bus, be able to take all of your stuff with you).

6. LEARN TO FORNICATE ON THE GROUND. This rule works well with #3 and #5. Nothing is worse than coming home to find your 57 square foot house rocking wildly from side to side—and don't even think of jumping in—something will get broken.

7. EVERYTHING IS EQUAL. If you eat together, buy half of the food. If a speeding ticket is acquired, half is to be paid by each party (assuming you were going to the same place). Nothing is more obnoxious than dead weight, and in the end, you're just trying to avoid being obnoxious.

8. BRING NO PETS. In a space that small, two is too much. Imagine returning to your automobile after an entire day of climbing to find the seats covered in poop, the door scratched, and a ticket on your hood in your name for your partner's dog (boy, did I catch hell for that).

9. BEAT THE HELL OUT OF EACH OTHER ON A REGULAR BASIS. This particular method of couple therapy only works if the two of you are evenly matched, but if that is the case, it's great. My friend and I looked like train wrecks toward the end of our partnership, but we never got along better. We got in fights in bar parking lots, poached hot tubs…. anywhere. We even got into a full-blown fistfight suspended a few hundred feet off the ground in the middle of a wall.

10. IF ALL ELSE FAILS—OWN THE BUS. It is a hell of a lot easier to be the ejector than the ejected. Hitchhiking is fun only if that is what you meant to be doing.

If you follow these simple rules while you live with someone else in a bus, hell will still probably break loose, but if you adhere religiously to #10, you will be all right. Happy motoring, and good luck.

Hop, Skip and Go Naked

(but for god's sake don't talk to anyone)

The other day I was working late in the office and I'd told a friend that I'd meet him at the hole at Taggart, on the Weber River to go kayaking. I got out of the office at 4:30 (yes that's late for me) and had just enough time to high tail it over to my house to pick up my stuff and haul some ass out to the "Mighty Webe." I picked up my dry top, skirt, booties and helmet, stuffed them into my bag and jumped into the truck. I proceeded at high speed down I-80 toward Echo. Just as I was passing Coalville I got that horrible feeling that I'd forgotten something. I went through my mental catalog of all my boating paraphernalia. Skirt: check; helmet: check; drytop, paddle, booties and boat: check. It was just about then that I looked down and noticed my wardrobe. I was wearing my Park City casual business suit. I thought about what that meant, and it didn't take me long to figure out that I didn't have any shorts. Now if I had thought to wear (or even own for that matter) underwear, this wouldn't be a problem; but as it was, I was on the horns of a dilemma.

When I got to the hole, I found that I had been flaked-on by my friends, and therefore would be receiving no outside assistance. There were however, four complete strangers playing in the hole. I was thinking there were three things that would pose difficulties in this venture: Getting in, getting out, and the possibility that I would have to swim. I have been boating for a while now and I have gotten pretty confident in my ability to roll back up when I tip over in the boat—but I was still having second thoughts. What better time to have a lapse of skill than when I would have to swim my boat to shore bare-assed, and dump the water out of it while staring any and all strangers in the face with my good ole' brown eye.

I figured I'd risk it and decided the only way I'd get out of my boat in the river was when the rescue team pried my cold, dead ass from it somewhere around Morgan. I had had a few spins in the hole—everything was going great, when sure enough, I finally tipped over. Now you've got to realize that when play-boating, water inevitably leaks into your boat and the combination of the water on the foam seat and my bare ass made the whole rig a little slick, making setting up for a roll more difficult. I missed my first three rolls and was pretty much convinced that I was going to have to do the "swim of shame." It gets very shallow just a little bit down river and having your head dragging behind your boat makes it just about impossible to do anything but pull your skirt. I hit the fourth roll and saved myself from certain disgrace.

While I was having my personal little epic, two of the boaters took off leaving me and one other guy at the hole. We finished off the evening playing in the hole and didn't say a word to each other. I think that I was so shaken by my near miss, and feeling so self conscious about not having anything on under my boat, that he could sense the awkwardness of my situation without quite knowing what my situation was. Anyway, we ended up having to leave at the same time and after I had gotten to my truck, sneaking low through the weeds, and got some pants on, we finally introduced ourselves and shot the shit for a while. This poor guy was probably getting a very weird vibe from me while we were boating and now thinks that I'm just extremely BI-polar.

Oh well. My advice to you readers if you end up in a similar situation is not to pretend everyone else is naked (that could get really weird). Use your imagination and convince yourself that you are not, while remembering enough not to flash everyone at the take-out. Or better yet, remember your shorts.

Mike Reberg

Getting Snowed in the San Rafael Swell

Randy Johnson cleans up right nice. And that's been a problem for the environmental crowd as of late.

Like some character from a cowboy poetry reading, the anti-wilderness commissioner from down Emery County way is playing a role... passing himself off as a reasonable, salt-of-the-earth cowboy trying to find compromise on the thorny issue of public lands conservation.

And he's been doing a good job of it too. He and Third District Congressman Chris Cannon, playing a similar character, have got a lot of jaded DC beltway-types thinking the San Rafael Western Legacy District and National Conservation Act, a bill that's winding its way through the halls of Congress, is something special; a new public lands middle ground.

Evoking the imagery of Butch Cassidy, a guy who outlawed his way around the San Rafael region 100 years ago, Johnson's even got the Interior Department folks sopping up the tall tale.

Interior Secretary Bruce Babbitt, desperate for a conservation legacy, is calling the measure a "wilderness neutral" first step toward real protection for the region. Southern Utah Wilderness Alliance Executive Director Larry Young recently called the legislation voodoo conservation. Conservationists think the bill does more harm than good because it fails to protect over a million acres of wilderness-quality public lands in central Utah, and gives the BLM another four years to rein in off-road vehicles—the main threat to the area. Babbitt, playing his own role, is promising conservationists they will get their wilderness later on, down the road.

But not if Cannon gets his way. The bill is a probe of sorts for the two-term Republican, a first push in what conservationists believe is an effort to dismantle the 1964 Wilderness Act. He is promising more of these "wilder-less" bills in the future, and Babbitt, a lame duck secretary, won't be around to demand future wilderness designations.

The San Rafael Western Legacy District and National Conservation Act is designed to deceive. The legislation is a lot like the temporary personas of Johnson and Cannon.

But the Utah Wilderness Coalition, a 181-member coalition, has spent a great deal of heart and soul trying to protect Utah's spectacular desert landscapes. It knows what's good, bad and ugly even if Bruce Babbitt doesn't. This one's bad, and the environmental community has seen too much of the real Johnson and Cannon to be fooled.

As an example, Johnson recently told a Christian Science Monitor reporter that the San Rafael Western Legacy and National Conservation Act was a "way around wilderness, because wilderness is a problem not a solution." So much for the "wilderness neutral" concept he has touted. He claims his words were taken out of context, but Johnson has an anti-wilderness press record as long as a Butch Cassidy rap sheet.

Cannon too, has toned down his typical anti-wilderness rhetoric in hopes of roping an election-year coup. A fat chunk of pork-barrel on a re-election brochure would look good to the folks in Emery County, never opposed to welfare if it's going their way. But who can forget Cannon's classic shoot-first-ask-questions-later stunt last spring when, following an anti-wilderness rally, he led a group of hootin' ORV riders into wilderness quality lands off-limits to motorized vehicle use. Documented in Utah newspapers, it was likely an illegal act, and Cannon knew it.

So here's why the San Rafael Western Legacy District and National Conservation Act has the conservation community concerned. First, the bill creates a national conservation area (NCA) around one million acres of the San Rafael Swell region, located within the boundaries of Emery County, and forms a "Legacy District" around an even larger area of that county.

The boundaries alone should tip off the suspicious. The true San Rafael Swell, a unique region of slot canyons, painted badlands and sandstone reefs, knows no county lines. The Swell region is one of the most easily definable geologic areas in all of Utah. This NCA, conceived by Johnson and introduced in Congress by Cannon early this year, conveniently lops off the Swell at the Emery County line, leaving out important regions of the San Rafael that need protection.

The reality is the legislation has more to do with a $10 million federal government subsidy, slated for Emery County, than it has to do with conservation. Johnson plans to promote tourism, including motorized recreation, in Emery County and

doesn't want to share his slice of the pork pie.

And that is another problem with the bill. Illegal off-road vehicle activity has skyrocketed in the San Rafael Swell. Like an ecological cancer, it spreads with every warm weather weekend. Cannon's bill fails to adequately address damage created by irresponsible off-roaders. In fact, the bill proposes to study the issue for four years. Meanwhile, Johnson plans to promote his county as an ORV destination, and without immediate and critical protections, pristine wilderness quality lands will suffer.

Finally, Cannon's legislation fails to designate any wilderness in the San Rafael Swell. The Utah Wilderness Coalition has identified 700,000 acres of pristine desert country within the proposed NCA boundary deserving of wilderness designation, a million acres if you include the entire Swell region. Two years ago Cannon offered an anemic 140,000 acres of wilderness when he sponsored similar legislation that was opposed by the Clinton Administration because it failed to adequately protect the area.

But since then, the Clinton Administration has been roped, tied, and branded. Ironically, Cannon played a big part in that. And in his mad, late administration dash to secure a conservation legacy, Babbitt has hitched himself to Cannon and the San Rafael Western Legacy District and National Conservation Act wagon. After all, it's got a nice, down home ring to it.

And that's the art of deception. You've got to give him credit. Randy Johnson cleans up right nice.

In the San Rafael Swell

Illustration by
Brad Wolverton

Now that's what I call conservation

Running a Little Smack at Hansen and Cannon

It is the sporting season, if you haven't already noticed. We've got it all right now...post-season baseball, pre-season basketball, hockey underway, and football in full swing (as a long suffering Rams fan I'm basking in these days). We're even wallowing in an Olympics afterglow here in Utah. Or is that a Fosters hangover?

I like sports. Sports, at their core, are easy to understand. There are winners and there are losers. Go 0 for 4 in a critical major league baseball post-season game, people are going to run some smack at you, and it doesn't matter if you're going to the Hall of Fame. Just ask Berry Bonds. Ask Karl Malone for that matter.

I used to write sports. I used to write about winners and losers. Sometimes losers lost with more dignity than winners won. Sometimes, losers blamed everyone but themselves...

...kind of like politics, which in a lot of ways is like sports. It comes down to winners and losers. Some politicians lose with dignity. Sometimes they throw their bat.

Which is a long lead in to what I want to talk about. Political losers. Sore losers. You guessed it. I want to talk about Jim Hansen and Chris Cannon, a couple of bad losers. But I don't just want to talk about them. I'm going pay a little homage to this year's autumn sports orgy and to my sportswriting roots...roots

deep enough to remember a time when Jim Hansen wasn't in Congress. I'm going to run a little old-fashioned, sports-style smack their way. They deserve it. They've been talking trash all year long. And when it comes to the San Rafael Swell, they got nothing to show for it.

Four times this season, Cannon and Hansen brought their San Rafael National Conservation area to the political plate in Washington D.C. Four times they struck out. That's 0 for 4. That's a zero batting average. If they were playing for Tony LaRussa, they'd be riding the bench, or worse, they'd be back in double-A. If Hansen, as chair of the National Parks and Public Lands subcommittee, is the committee's coach, Republican leadership ought to be calling for a coaching change.

A few days ago President Clinton signed the $18.8 billion Interior Appropriations Bill into law. It was a compromise measure that passed both houses of Congress by wide margins earlier this month following intense negotiations by Democrats, Republicans, and White House staff. Only 69 members of the House voted against the compromise. Two of those no votes came from Hansen and Cannon. Why did they vote against the bill? Their poorly written, one-sided San Rafael National Conservation Area wasn't in the compromise spending bill.

That was their fourth loss, a whole extra out in a year-long San Rafael inning. It was a pathetic final defeat for two guys who over-hyped their ability to pass legislation without working with the conservation community. On the floor before the appropriations vote, Hansen bitched at his colleagues for leaving out his

San Rafael "rider" he so desperately wanted in the appropriations package. Then Cannon went to the local press and howled that the White House had backed off its support of the San Rafael NCA, leaving Cannon without a bat. Actually, the White House was probably throwing at his head, but I'll get to that in a minute.

I've mentioned the San Rafael Swell in these pages before. Back in June, Cannon and Hansen tried to dunk their poorly conceived NCA over the outstretched objections of the conservation community. At that time, Cannon did have the support of Bruce Babbitt and the Interior Department, and he and Hansen were running their own brand of smack during floor debate—telling their colleagues that only "environmental extremists" could oppose their bill. But on the House floor, Democrats and conservation-minded Republicans rejected Hansen and Cannon, calling Babbitt's support of the proposal a "bad deal for the American public," and began amending the bill.

It was a straight-up game; Cannon and Hansen lost. Punked in their own House, Cannon and Hansen pulled the bill before more amendments could be passed.

0 for 1 and looking for revenge.

Next they tried muscle and intimidation, and again ran smack in the press about it. This was a Hansen play, because everyone knows Cannon's got no juice on the Hill. Hansen, as a subcommittee chair, tried to jam up other members' bills, demanding a trade for the Swell.

Now, for muscle and intimidation to work, you've got to be a bad ass and you've got to have something of value. The San Rafael NCA lost a lot of luster when both Democrats and Republicans took it downtown. And as for being a bad ass, there are bigger ones than Jim Hansen in both the House and Senate. Hansen learned a lesson about messing with a Senate Republican bad ass.

0 for 2 and looking stupid.

Finally, and still talking trash, Hansen promised there was more than one way to skin a cat. A rider. A rider is a backhanded way of attaching bills to year-end spending measures. Kind of sneaky, but part of the game. But deals change with riders, and supporting bills straight up vs. supporting riders are two different things.

When Cannon howled to the press about losing White House support, he never really had it at that point. The White House had long ago made a trade; House Democrats for Cannon and Hansen. It was an easy trade. They'd already gone 0 for 2.

So, within 72 hours of announcing there was a San Rafael rider, it was out. Democrats didn't like it, the White House didn't want it, and Republicans, remembering their June embarrassment, didn't think it was worth the fight.

0 for 3. Hansen and Cannon didn't even take the bat off their shoulders.

In spite of their poor performance, Cannon and Hansen are talking about running the bill next year. But they've got to win reelection first, and Republicans have to retain a majority in the House. And in case they still don't know, the conservation community's got more game than Nintendo.

Getting a Handle on the Real Extremists

Like a buzzard waiting for death to arrive, Emery County Commissioner Randy Johnson eyed the floor of Congress from his perch in the House gallery. Our anti-wilderness cowboy commissioner had soared the jet stream all the way to Washington D.C. earlier this month to watch the conservation community put up its final struggle—a floor debate and vote on the San Rafael Western Legacy District and National Conservation Act—then die a legislative death.

Johnson, aided from the beginning by Chris Cannon and Jim Hansen, Utah congressmen rabid with anti-wilderness sentiment and Interior Secretary Bruce Babbitt's endorsement, was convinced he was there to witness the final breaths of the Utah Wilderness Coalition's opposition. The Coalition had been trying to improve the San Rafael Swell National Conservation Area legislation ever since Cannon offered it up in February. The coalition believed the bill provided too few protections for the spectacular and beloved region of central Utah. It was willing to support the bill, but only with changes.

Johnson, Cannon, and Hansen must have smelled victory. Hansen quickly scheduled floor time for the legislation just days before.

An easy day, they must have figured. A couple of amendment votes, about an hour's worth of debate, and the "environmental extremists" (plus a few misguided, rabble-rousing Democrats) would be finished, leaving Johnson to swoop vulture-like down to feed on the carrion—in this case a $10 million bonus appropriation for Emery County tucked in bill's language.

That's what Randy Johnson must have thought anyway. That's what most people thought. The conservation community had done all it could do, but Babbitt's support of the measure was like a gut shot to the coalition, and that had made passage of the San Rafael Western Legacy District and National Conservation Act seem likely. Smart money was on the one-two punch of the Republican controlled House and Interior's support.

So what happened during the next several hours was nothing short of incredible.

House Democrats didn't die. Joined by a small band of conservation minded Republicans, they started making the legislation better with amendments, supported by the conservation community. Not great amendments mind you, but amendments that would, on the front end, provide the Swell expanded boundaries, real protections against off-road vehicle abuse, and some protections for wilderness quality areas. Those protections, conservationists believed, were essential while a four-year planning process, mandated in the bill, took place for the region. But rather than accept those modest reforms, Cannon and Hansen pulled the bill from the floor. As this edition goes to press, the bill remains pulled.

At the Southern Utah Wilderness Alliance office, staffers

watching the entire four-hour debate on C-Span cheered. For some time now, SUWA and other coalition members have been labeled as "all-or-nothing environmental extremists" by Utah's anti-wilderness politicians, and by many editorial pages in the state. Mainstream Americans have never believed that. Mainstream Utahans don't believe it either.

It was, therefore, interesting to watch the contrast between those seeking real protections for the San Rafael Swell and those trying to pass the bill as is. Democrat after Democrat rose to speak with eloquence and passion about the need to provide real protections for the San Rafael Swell. Republican pitchmen like Hansen and Cannon spent their time reminding House Democrats that one of their own, Babbitt himself, supported the bill, and that the only groups opposed were "environmental extremists."

"Babbitt cut a bad deal," George Miller (D-CA) told his Republican colleagues; and Brian Baird (D-WA) who has probably spent more time in Utah's desert country than Hansen or Cannon said these words: "These areas we are talking about have a silence most Americans cannot imagine. It is a silence that is breathtaking, a silence that is awe-inspiring, a silence which must be preserved."

After the debate, Utah 2nd Congressional District Congressman Merrill Cook said he heard a lot of people complain about Hansen and Cannon's constant use of the word "extremists."

"When half the Congress wants more wilderness, you can't call that position extremists. You may argue against it, but you can't call it extremists," Cook was quoted as saying.

Cook is absolutely correct. A majority of the House of Representatives were ready to give the San Rafael Swell the protection it deserves. Democrats and Republicans, representing a huge cross-section of regular Americans, demanded a better deal for their constituents (after all, Americans are the ones who own America's federal lands).

As expected, some large Utah newspapers called the bill's defeat a missed opportunity, blaming the environmental community and its "all or nothing" approach. Unfortunately, that has become their typical provincial reaction to this national issue whether it is accurate or not.

The reality is that when the bill started to get modest on-the-ground protections for the land, Cannon and Hansen pulled the measure from the floor. And truth be told, Hansen had to twist a lot of Republican arms or the amendment votes would not have been that close.

On this national issue of federal public land preservation in Utah, Cannon, Hansen, and our Emery County friend Randy Johnson turned out to be the extremists. They wanted it their way or "nothing at all."

Andrew Haley

Why No Rye?

I must admit that I have a certain liking for whiskey that most people just don't understand. It's the kind of love that I could only explain to a small group of anonymous chain smokers. I'm not rich enough to be too snooty about my whiskey, but I'm not poor enough to throw all my standards out the window. Be it bourbon, Irish, Scotch, Canadian, sour mash, tin tongued, Tennessee, or Timbuktu—I'll drink it and I'll probably flash my patented whiskey grin.

Now I must say that despite what certain individuals might say, Irish whiskey is the best whiskey on earth. The drunk bastards invented it, and perfected it, all the way from stovetop jet fuel to 16-year-old single malt Bushmills (the best is Red Bush, of course). The only problem with Irish whiskey is those damn tariffs. Good whiskey goes down easy, and .75 liters isn't all that much. So dropping $20 on a bottle of Paddies or Jameson stings sometimes.

When I was a bit younger, I ran across an Irish bartender in the alcoholic wilds of the Alaskan frontier who agreed with me about the qualities and price problem of Irish whiskey. His solution was simple: go Canadian. A helluva lot of Irish ended up in the 51st state during the great potato dash, and while we sat on our thumbs during prohibition, they were busy working overtime to keep the underground whiskey train rolling.

It's true, Canadian rye whiskey, as well as the handful of rye whiskeys made stateside, are quite similar in flavor and quality to Irish whiskey; and thanks to NAFTA, they come at a lower cost. Now I'm not pretending to say that rye can replace Irish in anybody's heart, but if Kentucky Sour Mash Bourbon isn't what you're looking for, and you don't have $75 to drop on Glengefardigramme Single-Bullet Ten-Gauge Pheasant-Scented scotch, you might want to give rye a try.

The only problem is that we live in Utah, and the DABC doesn't import it. If you head down to the liquor store right now, you'll see 27 different inbred Tennessee distilleries, 39 platinum coated vases of scotch, a smattering of over-priced Irish whiskeys, and a few unidentifiables you last saw on your way to the floor in Hell's Tavern. It's always a problem when non-drinkers are put in charge of ordering all the booze imports for your state. It's like having a mechanic take orders from the bakery.

This is just a subtle hint to the temperate bastards of the DABC, WHY DONT YOU IMPORT ANY RYE WHISKEY!?! I understand that we may be at a tense moment with our northern neighbor over Cuban business prospects and the South Park movie, but even blue-blood shit-kickers like Jim Beam make a fine rye. It even comes in a handsome yellow label.

So then, until they do, I'll be crying in the aisles, waiting for deliverance. But hell, it's better than being stranded in a Russian submarine.

Something Stinks

I suppose that a few generations ago if our Guy Smiley governor had told us that we needed to cut a highway through miles of marshland right beside the one we had just finished, we'd all sit back and praise the lord for his guidance. Maybe because I saw too many journalistic thrillers and heard too many Watergate jokes when I was a kid, I have this nasty habit of saying, "Hmmm?"

Let's ask ourselves some questions? Why would a good 'ole boy like Mike Leavitt want to build a second, north-south highway right beside the existing one? Sure, traffic's only going to get worse, but why didn't we just build I-15 wider when we had it shut down? And why build the Legacy Highway through a marshland? We live in the middle of nowhere folks. Come on! There's got to be some other route that's not going to piss off SLCACEEPA, or CALSPEACE, or ENVIRODRED, or whomever.

Anybody who's seen China Town knows that the first thing to ask when weird things show up around the water is, "who's got something to gain?" So here's my bet: 'Ole Governor Smiley has a stake in this marshland to get that road built, 'cause a long time ago the lord said unto his friends, "Buy cheap land and the governor will provide you a highway." I think some nifty, young whippersnapper at the Tribune ought to go dig around in State records to find out who owns the land that the projected Legacy Highway off-ramps will go through.

Just imagine; you have friends in high places who are surfing the, "LET'S GO TRACTORS" Olympic vibe. You have a stack of cash higher than Moroni on roller skates. You buy a bunch of worthless, soggy dirt out by the airport and all along the lakeshore; because there's nothing out there, it's real cheap.

You drop your tithing in the right chute and, "Bam!," "The governor has a vision! A ribbon of oily crushed rock running to the promised land. Where once there were ducks, there will be shopping malls, gleaming 16-theater movie complexes, stumpy office buildings with thousand unit parking lots, and over it all, the great throbbing green light of money!

This whole Legacy Highway thing stinks of the same high-level hand jobs that tore out the trolley lines, built the Triad Center, and sold huge tracks of National Forest to Snowbasin so a bunch of Nigerians could race down it for two weeks in 2002. It stinks of white-collar crime that gets ugly, useless things thrown up where they just shouldn't be. It stinks of the all the private donations, soft money, little gifts, and power lunches that have turned conspiracy into such a bad cliché that a dumb schmuck like me who doesn't even watch the news can smell a rat all the way out to the airport. Folks, its stinks even worse than the land their gonna build it on.

The only thing that amazes me is that the EPA actually said no, and the SLC Planning Commission said no, and that the Army Corps of Engineers might actually listen to them. There really must be a God.

What a Park-ing Garage!

Of all the groups of people in the world, and I mean every single one, no one, anywhere, has worse architectural taste than the Bovus Magnus Desereti, or common Mormon. The local legends are full of examples. Look at the Temple. Who are we kidding? The BBC made fun of it last month on international radio. They called it an eyesore. They don't have anything to lose. They don't have to live here.

Here's a Temple fact for you. Did you know they used it as a prop in the He-Man sequel: The Siege of Greyskull? And those blue-colored jackets that Temple security wears—my God! It's the same color as my friend's '84 Dodge Aries—after he drove it off the highway.

And then there's the new assembly hall. Whoever thought that you could ruin Fascist architecture? I wanna' know when the Jazz are going to start playing there instead of the Delta Center. Changes the meaning of Conference Champions, doesn't it?

But this new park they built on PUBLIC PROPERTY is an all-time low. Who in the name of God thought a dozen potted scrub oak would make that concrete soccer field look attractive? It was more inviting when a street ran through it. Those giant, stupid looking bird feeders look like diving pools for Moroni! The irony behind it, is that those big, stupid dishes were designed for the 2nd Fighter Wing of the Mormon Seagulls, but Rocky thwarted everything by declaring that since fuel prices were so high, the IOC would cut down on costs by using those stupid bowls and a few tons of pig shit for the Olympic torch.

The real jewel in the design is the giant hole in the parking entrance at the bottom of State Street. What a magnificent idea! Imagine the pastoral effect on visitors when they drive down from Idaho or Ogden for the ballet, or to catch the Jazz at the LDS Conference Finals. After hours on the road, imagine coming over Capitol Hill and heading straight down into that gaping keister snuggled between Castle Greyskull and the Amazing Office Building. What a treat!

The fact is, Mormons should not be allowed to touch a drafting pencil. Mormons should never, under any circumstance, be given access to cranes, dump trucks, or bulldozers (unless a dam breaks). Mormons should, above all, never be given the power to purchase pieces of our city.

You may think the old guys in the locker room at the Deseret gym were creepy. You may think that Main Street sucks from Lambs up anyway. You may think it's a bargain to sell off some rotten piece of town, but Jesus, look what they'll put up in its place! I thought we had Masons in town for a reason.

This isn't just joking around. I'm very serious. One of these days the Church is going to bid on North Temple between the Hinckley-Malone-Stockton Assembly Hall and Temple Square. They'll be very quiet and very persuasive.

Who knows what kind of slick arrangements will be made on high to get those public thoroughfares? But no matter the compromise, and believe me, we have a Legacy of compromise in this town, they'll try for it.

You see, when they bought Main Street and built that parking garage, it threw everything off by turning Mormecca into a rectangle. The only way they can turn Temple Rectangle back into a square is by buying all the streets surrounding Castle Greyskull. Imagine a concrete beltway linking all of those architectural felonies together.

But hey, Roman Catholics have their own country, so the least Mormons deserve is their own mall.

Predictions For The Next Thousand Years

Evening readers; Doctor Shiteeri Wamwami Bonzai here with my 2001 predictions—ah hell, with my predictions for the next thousand years. To start, let me apologize for my long silence. It has been a devastating season for all of us here at Transcending Mundane, Inc. Yea! even a heavy gloom of hopelessness has settled over the monastery as the Baboon King picks through his cabinet like a desperate sailor through a pride of rotten whores. I thought the Constitution had a clause preventing the possession of nuclear weapons by anyone too stupid to fail in the oil business.

Anyhow, to continue, I train my gaze at the brown diaper of a sky, and strain to see the future through our coughing pall.

So then, with a throw of the lever and twist of the magic sack, Dr. Bonzai begins!

PREDICTIONS OF THE NEXT THOUSAND YEARS

1. The note on my door that reads, "WARNING! THIS IS A NO SMOKING BUILDING. MY INSURANCE DOES NOT COVER SMOKING. IF I FIND EVIDENCE OF SMOKING NEAR YOUR UNIT AGAIN I WILL HAVE NO CHOICE BUT TO EVICT YOU" will be carved in the ozone by tiny flying robots made of aerosol cans so that everyone, everywhere with exposed skin will be burned to death by the rays of the almighty sun...

2. ...leaving by natural selection only members of the Taliban, and bureaucrats in cheap polyester suits...

3. ...who will immediately create new and improved death penalties for all sorts of social disobedience, especially all forms of environmental protest, questioning tax cuts, and the ownership of large dogs.

4. Carlos, the Mexican squatter who shares the bed with me and my girlfriend, will go on the road in a school bus, putting on brilliant theater for the impoverished (after he learns how to read). He will become the heir to Shakespeare's throne and the principal figure of a new religion, preaching humility, charity, and bawdy humor...

5. Carlos will be promptly executed by public blending by the International Talibanian Republic of God-Fearing American Bureaucrats for his hit musical "The BureauCats!"

6. The Bush family will annex all National Parks, National Wilderness Areas, and BLM areas, and transform them into

the international sensation known as Dubya's Oil World, where Micky Mouse will be publicly executed by forced drinking of crude oil, after he has publicly renounced his question, "Hey Kids!...hehehe...ever seen the Matterhorn?"

7. During the fifth anniversary festivities for Dubya's Oil World, Jeb Bush will spontaneously combust, burning down the state of Alaska and causing a hole in the ozone the size of India to form over the Northern half of the United States, which will be hailed as a "Giant leap for progress, science, democracy, and the American Way."

8. The genetic cloning of all cows, pets, soldiers, fruits and vegetables will accidentally sterilize the world food supply...

9. ...and the Federal Seed Reserve will turn out to be empty because the guards on duty "got bored" and "smoked that shit." As a result, the remaining bureaucrats and members of the Taliban will die out, except for the Mormons who are used to eating such crap that they take to eating sand, but only buffet style. But before the meaty paw of history interferes...

10. Tomorrow morning, once I get Carlos out of here, on each door in the building my landlady will post an impersonal note that reads: WARNING! THIS IS A NO FUN BUILDING. MY INSURANCE DOES NOT COVER FUN. IF I FIND EVIDENCE OF FUN NEAR YOUR UNIT AGAIN I WILL HAVE NO CHOICE BUT TO EVICT YOU, and I will get evicted.

Take Fifty Steps Back

In the new movie "Enemy at the Gates," the conflict between Hitler's German forces and the Red Army is distilled down to a sniper duel between two men. In the movie's version of the battle of Stalingrad, which (sorry Private Ryan) was the deciding battle of World War II, and hence the reason this isn't written in German—groß Gott! We see those oh-so-familiar German helmets off in the distance, shooting and shouting at the poor sickly looking Russians to surrender.

In the movie, surviving the German siege requires nothing but hope, and hope requires a hero—in this case the hottest English bloke in Russian history, Vaseline Luvontop. "Do you know any heroes?" Khrushchev, who wasn't there, asks young Will Shakestein. And so it goes; Jude Law's face is passed around, everyone sighs, and the Russians win. This is, unfortunately, not how the battle, and thus the war, went. Complicated Russian military strategies, excellent timing, new equipment, brilliant tactics, and a bunch of administrative bungles brought the Germans down. But it took three years and more blood than the US army would know what to do with.

Ladies and gentlemen—or at least those of you who are warm blooded—we are under siege. Al Gore, who received the second highest number of popular votes in US history, narrowly lost his rightful place in today's newspapers and tomorrow's history books. This is not because of the millions of dumb crackers across the nation who would vote themselves into the electric chair; nor because of the far left who would vote themselves into concentration camps, but because of a former cigarette model, dying in senility, who once ordered National Guard troops to march on a peace demonstration with orders to shoot to kill—the only man who ever won more popular votes than Al Gore—Mister Ronald Reagan.

Reagan had the good fortune of stacking the US Supreme Court with enough fascist emissaries (who, by the way, recently voted in support of hospitals that turned over blood test results taken without the consent of pregnant mothers to the police so that the mothers of new born children could be thrown in prison) that his legacy has continued to this day. It was Reagan's Supreme Court that has given us our un-elected president—a man who couldn't make money in oil; a man who would have been executed by his own policies if he were poor, Latino, or not the son of a former CIA Director; a man who has the amazing capacity of making convicted killers look eloquent; a man who was not elected.

Our un-elected president has decided to repay his debts by ending a fifty-year policy of running potential federal judges passed the American Bar Association (the group of people who determine who is and who is not qualified to be a divorce lawyer) let alone a Federal Appeals Court judge.

During President Clinton's last years in office, the

Republicans in Congress prevented the appointments of over 100 Federal judges that Clinton had put forward. At the time, this may have looked like nothing more than a taunting, "fuck you" from those meek, petty worms of men who managed to impeach the most popular president in history.

But oh, we were wrong. Because of the blocking of these appointees, there is a major shortage of Federal justices in this Wal-Mart we call America. And fascists, like nature, abhor a vacuum. With a Republican Congress, a Republican White House, a Republican Supreme Court, and a disregard for the opinion of the American Bar Association, the lights are all green for Dubya to fill those cold courthouse chairs with the fat, delicate white asses of people even more conservative than himself.

So why should I give a shit, you're probably thinking.

If your daughter gets knocked up and needs an abortion; if you're found guilty of something you didn't commit; if you ever smoked marijuana; if you think that Darwin belongs in high school science classes and prayers don't; if you think banning books is ridiculous; if you think you should be able to trade songs online; if you know a gay couple that wants to get married; if you look at porn on your home computer; if you think chopping the cocks off of statues is a bit old fashioned; if you think art has a place in society; if you like breathing; if you want to go backpacking in the wilderness and not run into oil refineries; if you want your children to grow up without getting poisoned by industrial pollution; if you think democratic countries should elect their leaders; if you think a planet needs an ozone to support life—then you better goddam well give a shit. Judges have the last word in this country, and the battle over these issues will be fought in the courtroom and decided by judges.

We are under siege. Ronald Reagan's Supreme Court led to our present, un-elected president. This un-elected president will fill enough Federal judgeships to seriously retard the development of American law alongside the fresh new currents of American morals and America's tradition of freedom and individuality. We have neglected our duty to protect our rights and our futures. We let a complex Republican attack put us back fifty years because we saw it not as the complicated assault it was, but let it pass us by unnoticed—a vague character in an oversimplified melodrama. To break the siege, we need more than a pretty face to pass around; we need the grunt and gristle to shoulder out of America our unwelcome enemy.

It's going to be a long march to victory.

Jim Moran

Rocky Mountain Hollywood

The year was 1992. I was an 18-year-old punk living in Summit County, Colorado. My roommate, ski idol, and best friend, Justin Patnode, had gotten one of the spots to be a stunt double for the movie "Aspen Extreme." The problem was that Justin had torn his ACL a few days earlier. He had his heart broken by the injury, but he was still strong enough to tell the director, E.J. Forester, that he knew someone who could replace him.

E.J. was skeptical, and said "If he is really good he'll prove it at the try outs, so you can invite him."

I did not know anything about this. Justin came up to me and said that I had been invited to the tryouts for "Aspen Extreme." I was pretty successful that year, but being only 18, I was a touch nervous that this was a 16.8 million-dollar motion picture. The last thing that I wanted to do was mess it up. If I got the part there would be millions watching me, and I would really not want to look bad. I said, "OK, I will do my best."

The day of the tryouts came quickly, and I had no idea what they wanted to see. They took us all to Snowbowl on a bitchin' powder day. They told us all to go to the top and wait. I was amazed at the size of the camera. It was like a small car! There were guys on radios, cameramen, assistant cameramen, grunts, the director, and about six assistant directors—too many people it seemed. One of the assistant directors told us that they would send eight skiers at once, and check them out on the way down. He chose the people who would go first. I was one of them.

I thought to myself "OK this is a big deal. I will go really fast at the beginning to get in front, then I will try to show my stuff." It was a small plan, but at least I had one.

Bang! We were off; I wasn't messing around. I skied as fast as I could to get in front of the pack. Then I saw a great air right on the first knoll. I pulled a huge double spread eagle. I was still going very fast. I decided to show them my diversity with few controlled, carved turns. I decided to straighten them out, and rip up a bump line. I threw two more huge tricks, then changed back to carved turns. Last, I saw a huge air right in front of the director's chair. I hit it hard, and hucked a huge, floating helicopter. I landed five feet from the director, hit my brakes and stopped dead in front of him.

"Hey Jim, you can relax kid; you got the part," E.J. said to me.

"Awesome Jim," Justin yelled. He had made the trip up on a snowmobile to check it out. I still hadn't figured out why they were so excited. I looked back up the hill. The other seven guys were only about half way down.

E.J. explained, "Jim I wasn't sure of your talents. I had to see for myself. You have the second unit spot to play Dexter. You will have a few weeks off. Then we will begin with the filming. I will see you in Aspen."

Justin was so proud, but he would have to wait for two weeks for me to leave for Aspen.

Aspen Extreme: #Part 2

The two weeks had passed fast, and it was time to film the movie. I won't lie, I was scared as hell. I made the trip to Aspen and stayed at a friend's house. My first day was an interesting one.

I showed up at the set barely knowing which way was up. E.J. was busy, so he told me he would see me later, and to follow the directions of Tom. Tom was a cool guy; he told me to go over and eat something at the food truck, and that he would be right over.

At the food truck, the cooks told me that it was only for the second unit. After a tedious process to confirm my role, they made me whatever I wanted. That made me feel kind of cool.

After I ate, Tom came over and directed me to the hairstylist to get fixed up. The stylist gave me a little dye and a trim. Tom then directed me to go over to wardrobe to get my clothing. I was shocked at the beauty of the wardrobe lady. I ogled as she set me up. Tom then directed me to jump in the limo and head to the mountain.

I finally made it up onto the hill to see that all the directors were still running around and setting everything up. They had a tent set up for the second unit. I was starting to feel kind of special. I grabbed some coffee and waited.

The time for the shoot finally arrived. We were all supposed to be trying out for the Aspen Ski School in a giant bump field. My job was to ski well in order to make Dexter look good in the film. All I had to do was ski a bump field—which was something I did all the time. The person playing T.J. was named Scott Kennett. We skied right next to each other and tried to look as good as we could while everyone else skied around us. Scott threw a huge heli-spread, so I decided to throw a big 720. All in all, the run went very well. Like all Hollywood films, they made us do it three times. The film crew was paying me very well, but that was all they wanted me to do that day.

The next day started out the same with the food truck, then makeup, wardrobe, and the limo ride. The shoot was different because I was supposed to be a ski instructor teaching a really fat guy. My job was to ski backward holding his tips. He was supposed to be so heavy that I couldn't deal with it. Then my job was to fall so that he would go out of control, skiing through the streets of Aspen until he hit a car.

This kind of action went on for a few days. We filmed the simple parts like freeskiing shots and the "powder eight finish." While we weren't shooting, we might have had a few parties with the actors too.

At the end of the week, EJ came up to me to make a proposal I could not turn down.

"Jim we really like what you have been doing. We had Scott Schmit and Doug Combs do the Powder-8 sequence up in the Monashees, but a lot of the filming didn't turn out. We were wondering if you and Scott Kennett would go to

Telluride with us to do a few small segments to put the film together."

I said, "OK E.J., that sounds good to me."

"I hope you are not afraid of helicopters, because we will have to fly into the backcountry," he said.

I had never flown in a helicopter before. Not only that, but they would pay me to do it! I agreed and we met in Telluride a week later.

I was so excited that the time just flew by. We all were supposed to meet at the IceHouse. I did not know it, but this place was the nicest hotel in town. I would get a minimum of $300 per day with a dinner per diem of $40. Every time I got airborne on my skis, it would be another $100. This added up quick. At just barely 19, this was a hell of a lot of money!

Scott was a Telluride local who knew all sorts of girls in town. He set me up on a blind date my first night. We had a blast dancing and drinking all night, but we had an early helicopter ride the next morning. We all called it quits fairly early (or I got shut down; I'll let you figure that one out).

The next day was a blast! I had more fun flying in the helicopter than skiing powder. They had us hit this small cliff three times, and ski some powder-8's. I started thinking this was what the rest of my life would be like. Heli rides, big bucks, and Pow Pow all day.

We spent the whole next day acting as the "Vail team" that crashes in the Powder-8 contest. The third day was a fun one too. They took us up to a steep section of backcountry to do some more Powder-8's. They also had me throw my heli-ironcross for a different scene in the movie.

Still to this day I love to watch Aspen Extreme. It was at the beginning of my fame in the world of skiing. And that was the easiest money I have ever made. E.J. called me the next winter. He wanted me to do the Schwarzenegger film, "True Lies." Even though I really loved doing Aspen Extreme, I had to say no. My dedication was in the direction of the Olympics, and nothing would stop me. But it's still fun to think about.

The Olympic Trial

The year was 1997; it was going to be 1998 in a few months. The US Ski Team said that for me to go to the Olympics, I needed at least one top-three finish, two top-fives, or three top-tens. I was not going to argue; this was the Olympics we were talking about. I had just gotten third at the Europe Cup, but it didn't count for the Olympic qualifications.

We were in Tigne, France and the World Cup season was just beginning. My first World Cup of the year did not go well. I didn't get my top-three. The tour would make the next stop at La Plagne, France. Things went better there, and I placed 5th. I only needed one more top-five to qualify.

The tour would make its next stop in Lake Placid, New York. The problem was that they had no snow, and the event would eventually get cancelled. The next event was one that I support, called the Gold Cup. The winner would automatically qualify for the Olympics. I liked the idea because whoever could handle the pressure would get to go.

I was ranked second in the U.S., but I flailed at the Gold Cup. A younger kid named Alex Wilson won and got his spot. The coach asked me if he could give away my spot to a younger skier. I agreed and he gave it away. This gave me only one other event to try to qualify through the team's ranking system.

I made the trip up to Blackcomb, British Columbia for my third World Cup. I ended up finishing 9th, but was still the second ranked American behind Jonny Moseley. I had not qualified through the U.S. Ski Team's system, but I missed two World Cup events. I had a meeting with my coaches, and they told me that if I didn't qualify under the Team's criteria, I did not get to go.

I told them that I was still ranked second, even though I missed two events. They didn't care. I told them that I had won two events, took three seconds and a third. I continued that I had competed in three World Championships, and definitely felt like I had a good chance to win for the U.S.

My coaches said that it didn't matter, and that I didn't get to go. My answer was quick and true. "I will see you in court."

I went home and got the best Lawyer I could find. His name was Ross Anderson—now the current Mayor of Salt Lake City. Ross could not believe that the US Ski Team did not want to send their best competitors. We discussed it, and I realized the importance of this case. I gave him all of my information and we filed a complaint.

Jim Moran and Rocky Anderson Take on the U.S. Ski Team

The time had come for legal action. I found an awesome guy to represent me, and you obviously agree because you recently elected him Mayor of Salt Lake City. The stress was high because this case involved myself and two other freestyle team members, as well as 23 alpine skiers.

Stacy Blumer, another plaintiff, had also hired a great lawyer who was young but obviously brilliant; Mark Levinstein graduated in the top of his class at Harvard Law School. We started out in a small meeting room. Our two lawyers decided that Rocky would handle the majority of the examining and cross-examining, and Mark would do the majority of the paper litigation. Stacy and I were supposed to shut up unless spoken to.

Right to work. The arbitrator entered the courtroom and introduced himself. Mr. Rowen, the lawyer for the US Ski Team, explained the reason for being there. Then Mark Levenstein talked about the necessity of the trial, and how the Amateur Sports Act states that the case is clearly justified. The first thing was to clarify the written material. The United States Olympic Committee had sent their lawyer to help out, but not take a side.

When it came time for the examinations, Rocky Anderson first called to witness Jonny Moseley (via telephone). They spoke about who he was and what he did. Then Rocky asked him if he felt that Evan and I had the potential to win a medal at the Olympics.

Jonny answered, "It is clear that their ability to podium is as good as mine, Alex Wilson, Jon Luc Brassard, as good as anyone. I know that because I have spent the most time with them out of anyone, and I've seen them perform in circumstances and win, and multiple times. I think that they have proven in the past three years that they have the ability to win. There is a lot of people who go through the whole World Cup on the Ski Team and never get close to the podium, and these guys came out in their first year on the podium. So that is where my feeling comes from; I wouldn't even be dealing with this arbitration if I didn't feel these guys could win the Olympics."

Next they examined Chris Haslock, then Liz McIntire, then it moved to Stacy's side of the examination. The first called was Matt Chojnocki. Mark Levinstein did this examination.

He asked Matt, "Did anyone tell you that there was a good chance spots would not be filled in the one allocated to the US Ski Team?" Matt answered, "No I thought it was kind of shocking not to fill the 14 spots."

Mr. Levinsein asked, "So basically on your understanding of the rules, and as a part of the team, no one gave you the clear idea before that, that was the likelyhood?"

"No. No it came as a surprise the other day."

Then they examined Bruce Erickson, a US Ski Team coach.

Mr. Levinstein asked, "Were you aware that there were complaints about sexual harassment in 1995 against Mr.

Hilderbrand?"

"Yes, I was aware."

"Against Mr. Hilderbrand?"

"Yes."

"Do you know if those complaints played a role in his being fired in 1995?"

"I am not the boss, and I am not making the decisions, but I am assuming so."

"Did you— do you know who made the decision with respect to Aerial Freestyle as to who would be given the discretionary spots?"

"To the best of my knowledge, no discretionary spots have to be given."

"Do you know who made the decision that no discretionary spots would be given?"

"I am assuming Mr. Hilderbrand."

The next examination went to Mr. William Joseph Stapleton.

"What is your present position with the United States Olympic Committee?"

"I am the current Chairman of the Athletes Advisory Council."

"And are you on the board of the USOC?"

"I am on the board, and the USOC Executive Committee."

"How long have you been on the Executive Committee?"

"Since 1992."

"To the best of your knowledge, has the— has there been discussion at the USOC about not sending every athlete to the Olympic Games that the USOC or a NGB permitted to send?"

"Yes, that has been a top group discussion for the past couple years."

"It had been an ongoing debate within the Olympic family. It was labeled 'The Full Teams Issue,' and the debate was whether we should still continue to do that, and there was a group of people who felt that it was part of— sort of the Olympic creed to take a full team, because it was about participation."

The examination of Joel Walsh was next.

"I am the athlete representative elected by the athletes of the US Ski and Snowboard Association to the Olympic Committee Athletes Advisory Council, which is a council representative of one athlete committee from an Olympic representative."

"Do you have a view as to whether Jim Moran is a genuine contender to win a medal if he were a member of the US Olympic Freestyle Team?"

"He most certainly is a contender."

"Does the approach of the ski association now, or the philosophy set forth particularly with regard to the Freestyle team, comport with that goal of the Olympic movement, and could you explain how?"

"It restricts the participation in the Olympics— in the Olympics arbitrarily, which not only affects the competitiveness of the team and the experience of the individual athletes who got to the competition, but it also cheats those people who those athletes come in contact with. It cheats the American public, other supporters of them, sponsors, and everybody on down the line who has any contact with the Olympics. Whether it just be watching in their living rooms on television, or knowing someone who went and participated, or knowing someone who might want to go and participate."

"So how would you characterize the overriding approach now of the Ski Association— with regard to the Freestyle Team?"

"IRRESPONSIBLE."

It was time for me to be examined. I started out by telling the story of my life and the fact that I have dreamed about representing the country in the Olympic Games. Then I gave the facts about my career.

"Can you describe for us here, what this means to you and— in your life?"

"Excuse me. I have a really hard time understanding the mentality of USSA. How I can devote my entire life to this, train every day, cripple my body, be qualified second— the second highest result on the US Ski Team and not have them send me, because they don't want to fill the spot. I can't understand that. And I will never ever understand that, never."

Then it was time for Bill Marolt. "Are you aware of what happened recently in China in terms of swimming competition and the world records that were purportedly broken by their swimming team?"

"Vaguely, I am aware of it."

"Are you aware that those records are not being recognized by the swimming association?"

"Uh-huh."

"Yes, I need a yes."

"Yes, yes."

"And do you know why that is?"

"Apparently they were taking drugs or— I don't know why."

"That happens when winning becomes everything, don't we see that in a lot in sports internationally, the use of steroids, the abuse of steroids, the use of drugs, anything to win— do you agree with that?"

Since Marolt's philosophy is all about winning, you can imagine his answer.

The final words of the arbitration were spoken by William H. Ericson.

"Accordingly, utilizing equitable powers, the arbitrators award that USSA and the USOC be directed to name Jim Moran and Evan Dydvig (mogul freestyle skiers), and Stacy Blumer (aerial freestyle skier), to be vacant spots on the US Freestyle Olympic Team for the 1998 Winter Olympics at Nagano, Japan. Costs are assessed against the respondent USSA."

The simple fact is that the US Ski Association was wrong. When the Olympics were first started, the founder, Pierre de Coubertin stated, "In idealizing participation and the struggle of competition over the fleeting glory of triumphs, I clearly recognize that for an athlete, the opportunity to compete is an important part of life."

He also believed that athletes striving for physical excellence demonstrated and developed moral and spiritual qualities that benefited society. The Olympic Games would contribute to harmony and peaceful relations among the peoples and nations of the earth.

Sending a team with open spots completely defeats the whole purpose of the Olympic Games. It had only happened once before in the history of the games. The common denominator, both times, was the Executive Director of the National Ski and Snowboard Federation, Bill Marolt. In 1984, the first time that this happened, he was the Head Coach of the Alpine Team.

When Marolt was an Olympian in 1964, he wouldn't have even qualified through the criteria that he made me try to accomplish. The fact is that this jerk does not even know what the Olympics are really all about.

My lawyer, Rocky Anderson, stated it best. "Your honor, we're talking here not about simple participation, because these extraordinary athletes who have been given the opportunity are going to make this country proud and are very, very likely not only going to make it into the finals, but have a great shot at bringing home a medal. But that is not the standard. The philosophy, apparently, of the Ski Association and of the Freestyle Team, and the philosophy set by the Ski Association only talks about winning. That is completely contrary to the entire Olympic charter and the goals of Olympism. The competitiveness, the fact that we are supposed to send our finest athletes is addressed in the federation statute. The Amateur Sports Act at section 374 (4), provides that the governing body which is— no, excuse me, that the United States Olympic Committee is to, and I quote, obtain for the United States the most competent amateur possible in each competition and event of the Olympic Games."

The fact is that not only did they f**k me, but they also f****d every citizen of the United States reading this. The US Ski Team has a lot to learn. The business world may revolve around money, but the Olympics does not!

You may hope that the US brings home the Gold, but for a moment, think about the bigger picture. The Olympics is about being the best that you can be and helping life evolve. It does not matter if the US is the winner. It matters that the human race pushes the envelope. I personally do not care who wins. It is more a question of did the athletes perform incredibly in the situation that they were given, did they push the envelope?

I learned a great deal. I was in a situation where I wanted to win and I had that goal, but more importantly my desire to achieve that goal was stolen from me. I was so happy that I won the case and they named me to the team that I simply lost my desire to win. Real true desire, the kind that combines your heart and your mind. I feel that I had the mind part, but the heart part was gone.

I quit the US Team because my heart wasn't in it anymore. My new goal became to prove that I was not just a "Bump Chump," and that my talents lay elsewhere as well. I had already learned the secret to life. I used it when I came out of my coma. My goal was to recover totally, and my desire was about one half a second behind. I still work on that goal today, and oh yes I still have the desire. Peace out!

The Road to Recovery

My skiing career came to a quick halt on February 20th of 1999. I suffered a traumatic brain injury competing at the U.S. Open in Vail, Colorado. I was in a coma for three weeks and in the hospital for seven months. Since then I have had to re-learn everything—to move my finger, to talk, to walk, even to blink.

I remember waking up and seeing nothing but the ceiling. I thought to myself, "I wonder where I am skiing today?" I sat up and immediately felt the weakness of my right side from the atrophy of paralyzation. Then I looked around me and saw that the room was completely padded, and there was no way out. I instantly knew that something was wrong. Then my mind made the connection: there is too much blue and white—I'm in a hospital. That was the first day of my conscious recovery.

In the days before, I had been talking to my mom, my dad, my brother and sister, and a few very good friends. How much of that do I remember? Zero, nada, none of it.

Do me a favor and wiggle your finger; now realize that your brain has as much to do with that as your muscle. You don't realize it until you don't have it, but your brain literally does everything.

My first lessons were the simplest of life's chores: speech, movement, writing. It may seem easy, but trust me it wasn't.

There were two things that helped me incredibly: 1) Physically, I was in great shape when the accident happened, 2) Most importantly, I already knew the secret of success!!!!

What is the secret of success? Well ask yourself this. What do all the best in the world have in common? Let's take Picabo for example; do you think she had a goal? Do you think she had the desire to win—true desire? The kind that combines your heart and your mind. Now let's take the best teacher in the world. Do you think that they have set a goal, and really truly desired that goal? I know the answer, do you?

When I realized that I was in the hospital and I was very seriously injured, do you think I used the secret of success? It took me about a second to use it. My goal was to recover totally, and my desire was about a half-second behind. I still work on that goal today.

I took my roommate's dog for a walk yesterday and tried to throw the ball for him. I threw it about 15 feet and it went totally a different way than I wanted it to go. For your knowledge, I used to be a pitcher so this disgusted me. Now I throw the ball all the time and I will until I get better. Like anything in life, your goals and desires are more important than you think.

Why is it that we only use approximately 7% of our brain? Do you know that we don't fully understand traumatic brain injuries? It is kind of the same statement in the form of a question. What will happen in the future? It is easy to look into the past. How much did we know about the brain in 1950 compared to 2000? How much will we know about the brain in the year 3000? Our brains are growing, how do I know that?

I think a lot about my brain these days, but only the things we use it for. Can you imagine what those are? Everything! Do you use your brain to write a speech? Well how about something more physical like walking? Reading? Cooking? Smelling? My point is that we use our brain for literally everything. Again, you don't realize it until you don't have it.

What do you write about when you write about the brain? I figured that I would do some research first, but all I could find was which part performs which function. Nobody in the whole world knows anything else.

I am still the same guy I was before the injury. What is it that I have gained, or lost from my injury? Well let's talk about the physical side for a moment. I used to jump on my skis a lot, and now with the risk of injury, I can't jump the way I used to. The second part that has changed is my realization of how close we all are to death. Does it really make a difference to the whole world if you die? Do me a favor and ask your brain that question for a few days. It is a simple question, but I can't answer it. The answer for humans and animals is evolution over long periods of time. It is the only thing that matters. Do you think we are evolving, trying to learn about something that we don't know about?

I survived a traumatic brain injury from the sport of skiing. The only reason that I am alive today is because I was wearing a helmet!!!!!

Thank you all for giving me a piece of your brain.

Mark Driver

Drunk, Vol. 1

It was a few years back in Indiana. I was in school. Craig, one of my old gutterpunk buddies who I hadn't seen in eight or so months, borrowed his new girlfriend's car and drove up from New Orleans to hang out for the weekend. He walked in the door with one piece of luggage: a 24 pack of Bud (of which five cans were already missing) and a bottle of generic tequila filled the empty space in the case. With a quick embrace, he set the drinks on my kitchen table and mouthed my sentiments exactly "let's get this beer out of the way so we can start the real drinking."

19 beers and 1/2 a bottle of generic booze later, we had caught up on just about everything there was to catch up on: who was married, who had herpes, who was in jail, and who was dead. It's amazing how you can go for a year without thinking about someone and then, upon hearing about his or her death, suddenly get crushed under a wave of sadness.

The liquor was taking its toll. We sat at my depressing kitchen table, bumming the hell out of each other with "remember whens" about our latest friend to get killed. By this point we were pretty cried out. My apartment was pretty dismal to begin with, add a couple of drunks with a sob story, and it became unbearable.

It was about nine on a Friday night in a college town. Kids across the city were charging kegs to their parent's emergency Visa cards. It was time to go out.

As luck would have it, the first party we went to was the all-nighter. An all-nighter doesn't necessarily have to last all night, it just means you don't have to supplement your evening by visiting other parties. They were tapping the keg as we tromped into their yard. It was October and the leaves were deep. The keg was in the backyard, conducive to evacuation in case of police raid (public intox=$140=no food). Out of our jackets we pulled 64 oz. Big Gulp cups we'd grabbed from my cupboard on the way out the door. We were already well beyond trashed, but it didn't matter. There's something about old friends that justifies drinking too much.

The party turned out to be the property of some guy I had a class with who I didn't recognize. He recognized me, though. He was a nice enough person, one of those mediocre people with lots of common sense. His friends seemed OK with us guzzling their beer, so there were no problems, at least not yet. Craig and I sat down in the leaves and talked old times, talked about where we were going, what we wanted to do, talked about who we wanted to fuck, and on and on, taking turns refilling the cups. Somehow it had gotten to be 11:30. The party was booming. The Pixies were fighting the Chili Peppers for the stereo, but we were so drunk that even the Chili Peppers sounded OK. It was my turn to get beer.

Craig yelled at me as I shambled to the end of the line, "don't wait in the line, just piss on those motherfuckers, they'll get out of your way."

"Of course," thought my poisoned brain, "piss your way to the keg." I had to go anyway. I dropped my pants/underwear combo down to my boots and started pissing on people. Craig was right; I wasn't going to have to wait in line. People trampled each other to get out of the way. I was almost to the front of the line, vaguely recognizing the disgust-tinged laughter (or laughter-tinged disgust) of the crowd around me as I watched my hand reach out for the black rubber, lifeline of beer. Suddenly, what remained of my peripheral vision picked up seriously aggressive movement to my right. I spun just in time to get tackled, but managed to get a clear shot at his face before I hit the ground.

I connected really hard, busting the glasses of the dick who had attacked me. Once on the ground, I rolled on top of him and headbutted him in the nose as hard as my impaired body would let me. The guy grabbed my throat and started squeezing, his face was bleeding and he was screaming my name.

"Driver, you dick"—oh shit—it was Craig! He was trying to keep me from getting my ass kicked, and got his nose busted in the process.

"Oh shit! Sorry, sorry, oh shit, oh shit, uh!" but what could I say? Even if my tongue worked, I couldn't say anything to fix his nose; Craig helped me out of my difficult situation by slugging me in the jaw and kicking my leg out from under me. The fight was on.

It didn't last for long. We got tired and just ended up collapsing in the mud on top of each other, laughing our asses off. Fuck, I don't think I ever laughed so hard in my entire life. We both laughed until he crawled into the bushes and started puking. My pants were still down. I pulled up my trousers, walked over, and found Craig's glasses twisted in the leaves like a train-wreck. Some girl yelled from an inside window "We called the cops!" I laughed again, found my good friend Craig in the bushes, and dragged him home. The only thing that got me home was the post-fight adrenaline. I think we tried to drink another shot in tribute on my kitchen floor, but I don't remember if I drank it or spilled it before my face hit the linoleum.

Eavesdropping on Lesbians

Last Friday, I went to see everyone's favorite one-lumberjack noise machine, Thrones. Waiting for them to come on, I was leaning against the bar, chugging beers and reading some hippie book from 1973 about how to hitchhike around North Africa: "always shave your head before entering Turkey— you can grow it back later." Hanging out at shows by yourself is sort of an art form that takes many years of practice. You need to give off the aura that "I'm by myself because I am only here for the music" or "I am by myself because frankly, other people bore me." "I don't have any friends" is probably more accurate for me, but self-pity rarely makes for good reading so I'll stop it there.

So anyway, I'm hanging out by myself and minding everyone else's business, because my book was starting to use words like 'groovy' and 'vibes' too much. A bunch of frat guys walk in and immediately mock some Goth kid sitting in the corner to make themselves comfortable. A girl and her date attempt to have a tender moment over plastic cups of Miller and a basket of soggy fries. Some woman with cleavage down to her knees and an ass down to her ankles caught my imagination for a few seconds, the dirty part of my brain devising combinations and permutations that could make even a congressman blush. Some 16-year-old looking kid chased his 16-year-old looking friend around a steel support post until the chaser tripped, bit it really hard, and tried to play it off like it he wasn't hurt.

Then this middle-aged, yuppie lesbian couple sat next to me at the bar. Imagine Susan Powder on a date with a flat-topped Janet from Three's Company. They smelled good but looked like they felt a bit out of place, like when you see parents of punk bands videotaping the show from the back of the room, elbow deep in surly teenage angst, trying to 'be cool,' but smiling a bit too much to be convincing.

The couple started up a drab conversation about some new, upscale brew pub that had a lot of promise: it was a good location and they had heard there was good food and how lucky they were to have so many good restaurants; how Seattle was supposed to have more restaurants per square mile than other cities—a statistic that pleasantly surprised the other one. Jeez, reading equipment-packing lists for North Africa seemed like a roller coaster on acid compared to these two yawn machines.

My attention passed to some guy with a Sonics sweatshirt, probably about 45, big bushy beard, big bushy gut, talking loudly, and laughing even louder in the face of two young girls he certainly shouldn't have been trying to have any sort of conversation with. He seemed to slowly realize that under normal circumstances, cute 21-year-old girls don't normally go home with fat, hairy men, and these circumstances were indeed normal. So he thanked them politely for ignoring him and stumbled over to the bar, where he saw my middle-aged lesbian buddies and, like a fat, bearded shark, moved in for the kill.

"Hello ladies," he started, "you're both looking lovely tonight. My name's Ron."

The women smiled painfully and said "hi" to Ron without introducing themselves, but that didn't seem to stop our buddy Ron. Oh no. Ron got a little closer to the blonde one. "So do you come here a lot? This is my first time. It's pretty crazy! Lots of beautiful girls!" They sat and sipped their drinks, half-smiling, looking beyond poor, drunk Ron.

All this was happening like two feet away from me. I pretended to read my book but was absolutely captivated by the scene unfolding; it was like watching a train plow into a church bus full of kids in slow motion. I couldn't look away from the ironic horror. I mean here was this guy, disgusting by anyone's standards, showing off the male traits that turn off most straight women—let alone lesbians. He was fat, drunk, loud, aggressive, and more than just a little bit stupid—completely hitting on these two women who had looks on their faces like an elephant had just taken a dump in their purses.

And yet, bless Ron's little heart, he was oblivious to it all; and man did he try. He tried so hard. He smiled, asked questions, made jokes, complimented, and he was getting nowhere. The women had completely stopped acknowledging his presence altogether, when he grabbed the blonde one by the arm and said "Hey!"

The woman jerked her arm back as if she had just accidentally dunked it in a gallon of sperm. "Excuse me!" she yelled, shocked and not quite sure what to do. Then, with their full attention, Ron glanced at his watch and went right for the jugular.

"I'm not drunk," he said with a suddenly calm face, "and I know you're both lesbians. I was just killing time until my ride showed up." And he walked off soberly, right out the front door of the club, leaving two shocked lesbians in his wake. I laughed, hard.

"Did, you know him?" the blonde one asked me, wide eyed and still looking confused.

"No," I replied, "but now I wish I did."

133

I Love Fags

I love fags. I don't like to make broad generalizations about a group of people as a whole, but I think they are some of the funniest, coolest, and nicest people the world has to offer. Especially impressive is their ability to be bluntly honest. I think the process from realization to the actual acting out of gayness requires a lot of self-honesty and soul searching that few of us straight fuckers ever go through. They understand, probably more than most of us, what it feels like to be unaccepted and hated on a daily basis. Few groups of people can be as viciously attacked without fear of public outrage as gays can be. They're easy targets, and any sign of compassion or attempts at understanding often puts you on suspicion of being gay as well, an accusation excruciatingly feared by most straight people.

The more time I spend hanging out with fags, the funnier I find people's reactions to homosexuality. Most straight guys, for example, think every gay male in the world probably wants them, as if being gay suddenly means that a person has no preferences or taste. In reality, most fags have way better taste in men than to come close to your hairy, jockey-shorted ass, and if anything, homophobic losers like you make them strongly reconsider women as alternatives (scared straight).

Even more interesting are the reactions of hardcore homophobes. Groups like the American Family Association and the 700 Club serve as watchdog groups to inform the world about the "Gay Agenda." These people seem pretty interested in researching the gay lifestyle, a little too interested if you ask me. It makes you wonder if they've even met an openly gay person before, or if all their impressions are based on their own perverted imaginations and fantasies. Kinda' like the people who want to ban all pornography; something has struck a chord in them and they can't just leave it alone like the rest of us; they have to ERADICATE it. Thou dost protest too much.

They even want to create a legal definition of marriage that keeps gays from getting married. The Defense of Marriage Act. Ha. Excuse me Congress, if you're gonna spend all my tax money trying to keep gay people from getting married, why don't you mail my share back. I can't even afford to get my car fixed and I don't give a shit what the legal definition of marriage is (jeez, talk about over-regulation). It's not like being married means anything aside from tax purposes anyway. Why not defend the institution of marriage from losers who represent the 50% that end in divorce? As the joke goes, if they really want to stop gay sex, they should let them get married; married people don't have sex.

One benefit of living in LA is that you get the dirt on which macho he-studs are into other macho he-studs, and I have news for all you girls lusting over your precious entertainment idols: THEY ARE ALL GAY. Heart throbs from "Saved by the Bell" to "90210" to "Friends" are smooching it up on club floors with members of the same sex. I won't name names, because it's funnier to keep you guessing, but you would die of shock if you knew about some of the unlikely couples I've seen. Which just goes to show you how bullshit our perceptions are when it comes to things we haven't experienced first-hand. Very rarely does the image mirror reality, so I suggest that you improve your reality base and take advantage of the resources homosexuals have to offer. Who knows, maybe you're gay and you don't even know it!

Government Defined

Government: A group of elected and unelected officials you pay to make decisions for you that you'd never make for yourself.

The President: A basically useless position remarkable only in its use as a diversion from real government incompetence. Put into place by billions of dollars, winners are usually those perceived as the most easily influenced by the majority of a specific persuasion, and in the case of a close race, the candidate most people would choose if forced into a sexual situation. Once a president is elected, his job consists mainly in fighting allegations made by the people who voted for his opponent. Any progress made during the term of a president should be considered accidental, and can usually be attributed to a naïve group of individuals actually taking a president seriously.

The Vice President: While the name might infer a less moralistic president, the vice president is instead chosen for his ability to be even less remarkable than the president. As you might imagine, finding such a person is no easy task.

Congress: A body of government employees, usually incapable of ethical individual enterprise, whose main concern is diverting money of working individuals to non-working individuals while diverting the money of corporations into their own pockets. Congress consists of two bodies, equally incompetent:

The House: A pillar of democracy whose main service to society is filling the airwaves with negativity during election campaigns that end briefly on the night of the election, and begin early the next morning. The main responsibility of the House is to painstakingly create laws that harm everybody equally, and send those laws to the Senate to be destroyed, or in the case of a particularly devastating law, passed.

The Senate: A group of adults mainly concerned with the fact that they haven't yet been able to secure their positions for life, although they are able to depend on their consistently mediocre performance to be re-elected by their consistently mediocre constituents. When not arguing the issue of increasing their own salaries, or determining the benefits-packages of their pensions after a glorious career of imposing on the freedoms on their countrymen, the Senate busies itself with not passing laws set forth by the House, or in the case of a particularly devastating law, passing it.

Speaker Of The House: An exceptionally skilled liar whose main function is coordinating attacks on the president, or if the president and the speaker are of the same party, making excuses for him. Recent speakers of the house have been required to possess a certain silver-haired Fred Flintstone quality.

Two-Party System: A brilliant illusion craftily manufactured to give voters the feeling of choice; choosing between the parties is like choosing between being slapped with the

136

front or the back of the hand.

Minority Whip: No one is actually sure what the Minority Whip is, although it presumably reflects Congress' attitude toward minorities.

Supreme Court: An office held for life, ensuring mistakes of the past are repeated for at least 20 more years.

State Government: An entity created for its ability to more specifically oppress you and your neighbors. Main duties include standing in front of citizens and charging to get out of the way.

Local Government: An entity created to make sure you can't park in front of your apartment, that you are duly punished for owning a house, and ensure that your children remain stupid enough not to clean up the messed-up town they are inheriting.

Taxes: 1) Punishment for working. 2) Good money after bad. 3) Inefficient fuel for an incompetent engine.

CIA: Noam Chomsky said that government is the shadow of business on America. It only makes sense then that the CIA is the shadow of American business on the rest of the world.

FBI: The thin blue line between you and the horrors of video-tape duplication.

Pollster: An unbiased, scientific sampler of public opinion who comes up with a precisely accurate account of exactly what sort of lies people like to tell nosy strangers on the phone. Polls have twice the political weight of any given public vote, and final accuracy of any poll can be judged by whether one agrees with it or not.

The Curious Fate of Nitro Villechaize

Intimidation is a curious thing. There was a little guy that went to my high school who was quite a bully. He'd strut down the halls shoving, and yelling, and tormenting, and punching. No one could really remember why he was justified to be such a bastard, yet no one would ever fight back. It was assumed that anyone acting as such is doing it because they can back it up with fists, knives, or guns. Successfully analyzing a bully as one blessed with minimal powers of personal introspection, acting out feelings of inadequacy and insecurity is a good pastime while you stay in the hospital. One day, another little guy, a new kid not smart enough to stay away from the bully, stood up to him and beat the fuck out of him. The spell of the bully was broken for most of us, which taught me an important lesson: to be intimidated, you must first believe.

One rainy Saturday in New Orleans, we decided to find a town with a stupid name and take a road trip to it. Cheesequake, New Jersey, and Truth or Consequences, New Mexico were too far away to make on one tank of gas, so we went to Hernando, Mississippi, a nice little hell hole a bit south of Memphis. The AAA guide said they had a Motel 6, a liquor store, and a Popeye's Fried Chicken—three elements sure to make any overnight trip a successful endeavor. Me, Lester, Ed, and Martelle all hopped into a bashed-up old Duster and hit the road; our luggage was no more than a crumbling cooler full of sodas,

beers, and gas station ice. A box of tapes wedged between the glove compartment and the floor mat meant that riding shotgun was devoid of its usual superior legroom, but other than that slight inconvenience, things couldn't be better. Riding in a car filled with best friends and good music is one of the nicest things about being alive. It's also a sure fire way to get in trouble.

We hadn't quite gotten to Hernando yet, but we were getting antsy. Ed was trying to load a squirt gun with bongwater, spilling most of it on himself in the process, and Lester kept trying to light the back of my hair on fire. Martelle had to piss, so we pulled off the highway into a town that had a sign for a university. I won't say which one, because we fucked a lot of shit up there, and I don't want it coming back to me, but let's just call it Michael Bolton University.

MBU, as it turned out, was a religious school that focused primarily on musical studies, seminary skills, and Phys Ed. We learned this by parking the Duster and walking into the student union where a rack of pamphlets explained everything. The place was sparsely decorated—a junk food machine, some flyers for campus revivals on the walls, and a semi-circular couch centered around an old television. There wasn't a lot of activity for a Saturday afternoon, just some guy sitting on the couch with his girlfriend watching Alabama play Auburn, which I vaguely recall as some sort of Southern rivalry, but I try not to retain that sort of information. The guy was really into the game, and the girl looked bored, at least until we walked into the room. Her look of boredom turned into slight panic as she nudged her boyfriend's attention in our direction. For a second they shared the same grief-stricken look, as if Mongols had broken down the drawbridge and were set to start pillaging. Lester picked up on their fear like a dog, walked over to the couch, and sat next to the guy. I sat on the other side of Lester.

The guy looked like a mixture of Nitro from American Gladiators (then the only television show that could hold our attention other than the Simpsons and Cops) and Herve Villechaize a.k.a. Tattoo from Fantasy Island. He was bulging with muscles to be sure, but at 5 foot 5, I suppose he felt he had to be. He had a crewcut and a whisper-thin mustache, a species that seems to grow best in the climate of America's Deadly Triangle (Alabama, Mississippi, and Arkansas). The girl was kind of cute, black shoulder length hair, wearing a gray Alabama sweatshirt. The pickings must have been pretty slim at MBU for her to settle for this guy. Maybe he had some personality going for him, but making your date sit though more than 10 minutes of football is up there with vomiting on yourself as far as turn-ons go. There was a long uncomfortable silence before anyone spoke; we stared at him and he stared at the TV.

Lester finally broke the silence. "So who's winning?"

Without even looking away from the screen Nitro answered. "Bama."

"Are you guys hungry at all?"

"No."

Lester shouted across the room to Ed who was doing pull-ups on the vending machine. "Hey Ed, get this guy a Twinkie!"

Ed fished through the change in his pockets and pulled out enough to make a Twinkie twist and fall off the metal spiral into the plastic staging area. He tossed the Twinkie across the room to Lester who unwrapped it and offered it to Nitro.

"I don't want it."

"Aw, c'mon. Eat it."

"I'm not hungry."

Lester's eyes narrowed and he got a bit more forceful. "Eat it."

It was Nitro's turn to narrow his eyes. He sized up Lester, took the Twinkie, and slowly, painfully ate it.

Lester watched him eat. "Hey Ed, I think this guy wants another one."

"Jeez, what a pig, but if he wants another one, I'll get it for him."

Lester unwrapped it and handed it to Nitro. "Eat it."

I suddenly realized what was happening—The Force Feed. It was a mean trick. Between Lester and Ed, they would get you to eat yourself sick before you knew what happened. They got me with it at their apartment once, when I first started hanging out with them. Half a sandwich here, couple pieces of pizza there, a candy bar, a tray of cookies, nachos, and pretty soon I was feeling like total shit. Everyone started laughing. "You fucking pig. Why stop now? Let's go get you some dinner, our treat." Yeah, good joke, but not always lighthearted.

"I don't want to eat any more." Nitro was putting up a pretty flaccid defense for one so buff.

"More? You want more? Hey Ed, he wants more!"

I counted six Twinkie wrappers on the ground. Nitro was turning green. Interestingly enough, his girlfriend was getting a bigger laugh out of it than we were. Cool girls are quite refreshing in the Deep South, where most women are convinced that their entire purpose on this Earth is to go to church and make sure their men get to work fed and go to bed laid.

"I'll take one," she said.

Lester smiled. "See buddy, your girlfriend can take it. What's your name girlie?"

"Don't tell him." Nitro tried his best to sound authoritarian with frosting caked on his lips.

"Amy."

"Hey Ed, Amy here needs a Twinkie."

"This machine is out of Twinkies. Sno Balls or Orange Cup Cakes?"

Amy answered "Cup Cakes."

Ed tossed and Amy caught. She opened the package and offered one to Nitro. "No, I don't want it."

"Eat it."

Nitro ate the cupcake, and got up to leave. "Fuck this. You can stay with these guys if you want."

"You're not going anywhere." Lester grabbed him by the back of the shirt and pulled him back over to the couch.

"C'mon Lester, this is getting boring. Let's go."

"No way man, this guy's still breathing."

"Remember what happened to the last guy," Martelle said, not even looking up from a pamphlet about the avoidance of sin and the advantages of healthy living he was reading in the corner.

"Yeah Lester, the Diabetic Coma Guy," I added. "Remember how messy that got?"

"Yeah, but that guy was sick to begin with."

"Kicking the shit out of him afterwards didn't help either."

Nitro's eyes were getting wider and wider. Lester turned to Amy. "What do you think?"

Amy thought about it for a second. She looked at Nitro, probably wondering if he had it in him to eat any more, wondering if she should punish him for whatever abuses he had dealt her in the past, wondering what things would be like after we left and it was back to him and her. She let the moment get painful, let Nitro twist and wiggle on the end of Lester's hook. "Can we stop watching football?"

"Yes."

"OK, he's done eating."

"If you say so," Lester let go of Nitro and smacked him on the back of the head. "Hey man, are you gonna leave all those wrappers lying around? What a pig!"

We piled back into the Duster and hit the highway. At some point Amy had given Lester a crumpled piece of paper with her phone number, which he uncrumpled and showed off with a huge grin. Lester actually drove back to the school a few months later and stayed with her for a week, but I don't think it amounted to much more than a few nights of sex and a couple dozen donuts. As for the rest of our trip to Hernando, it must have been fun because I don't remember a thing.

Al Fonzarelli

Missionaries Are Packin'

In response to the terrorist attack on the United States, Mormon Church President Gordon Hinckley has ordered all missionaries, both domestic and abroad, to arm themselves for the purpose of self-defense.

Church spokesperson Dale Bills said effective immediately, all of the estimated 57,000 Mormon missionaries worldwide will be issued a specially constructed Book of Mormon where a hollowed-out portion of the book conceals a 10 shot, 40 caliber Beretta automatic handgun.

Said Bills, "We are taking the necessary precautions to protect the thousands of brothers and sisters who serve the church throughout the world. We have decided to conceal the weapons in the Book of Mormon as opposed to wearing the sidearm in a holster. We think this is both prudent and practical—prudent because we live in a new and dangerous world—and practical because we do not want to alarm those we witness-to by pointing a weapon in their face. Also, since the holy book is always in hand and at-the-ready, our missionaries can more easily access their weapons and more rapidly fire upon the enemy. If church founder and prophet Joseph Smith had such an ingenious tool, he may have been able to surprise and overcome more of the guards at the jail that housed him, shortly before a breakout attempt that resulted in a shootout and his death."

When asked what conditions must be present before deadly force can be used, Bills replied, "All our missionaries must feel their lives are in imminent danger before they are authorized to use deadly force. Or, if they come upon information or believe that a member of the church is not obeying the commandment of tithing, they are to visit that member and open to the appropriate page of the book, if you will, and remind them the Lord is a jealous god."

Apparently the issuance of side-arms to missionaries is not the only change being instituted by the Mormon Church in response to what are suspected to be Islamic terrorists attacks on the United States that have left more than 5,000 dead.

The normally serene and tranquil grounds of the Mormon Church's Mission Training Center in Provo, UT, is now a place where on any given day, sounds resembling basic military training can be heard from afar: sporadic gunfire, mortar explosions, and young missionary cadets singing cadence as they march to Mormon Mission Drill Instructors.

In downtown Salt Lake City, future venue of the 2002 Winter Olympic Games, Mormon Church security has increased its presence and has undertaken measures to defend church headquarters and the Mormon Temple from a possible terrorist attack. The deafening sound of bulldozers and backhoes tearing up concrete can be heard around church property as they make way for installation of anti-aircraft artillery posts.

In addition to casting out those who use vulgarity, wear tattoos, listen to music, smoke tobacco or are perceived as a menace, church security guards now routinely expel anyone wearing a turban or a red dot on their forehead from their property and future site of the Olympic Medals Plaza.

Snoop Doggy Dogg Converts

Gangster Rapper Snoop Doggy Dogg, whose platinum records include "Serial Killa" and "For All My Niggaz & Bitches," announced today he is terminating his recording contract with Death Row Records to serve an LDS Mormon Mission in Salt Lake City, UT.

Elder Dogg, accompanied by his mission companion, arrived for an interview at Sizzler's Restaurant on 400 South in Salt Lake City dressed in a white shirt and missionary tag.

In an informal question and answer session with reporters, Elder Dogg was uncharacteristically reticent but upbeat. "Y'all think I'm running some kinda shit here, but this is the real deal."

Apparently Elder Dogg received his mission call from none other than LDS Apostle Neal Maxwell.

"I was hanging with my boys getting high in the Dogg Pound and my pager goes off. I didn't recognize the area code 801 so thinking it was business, I call the number and it was Brother Maxwell, for real. He tells me to stop hitting my blunt for just 10 minutes and hear him out. So he runs this bit on me about God's plan for my life."

With tears welling in his eyes, Elder Dogg continued, "I told him, 'look nigga, I don't know you from shit. All the apostles I know is dead. Just maybe God wants me to die in flames as a message of salvation for other motherfuckers watchin my ass.' Then Maxwell says 'Brother Dogg, Tupac messed up and now he's takin the big dirt nap and that's his gig, but God's got you scheduled for a different party and if you really want to help Shakur, you can baptize him once you're in with us. Besides, we need you to bring a little color here to Salt Lake.' So I told him, 'Count me in nigga.'"

Elder Dogg doesn't plan to perform or write any new songs so he can devote his efforts to the mission field. However, Elder Dogg broke into an impromptu performance of his last rap song aptly entitled "Mormonz In The Hood":

Niggas chill cuz the temperature is droppin,
Like a motherfucka's ass that my Glock is clockin,
Your body and your souls are in an invisible prison,
From druggin and consumin the white man's vision,
Of what niggas is and ain't so you don't have no ambition,
And so you can die in the nigga tradition.

So you motherfucka's thinkin I'm some kinda phony,
I'm about to break it off in your ass with my testimony.
Now I can dig the cash, the bitches and Benz's,
But you can keep your shit if you mend your fences.

My homeys in Salt Lake City got lots of ride and gash,
And those whiteys can teach you niggas how to pile up cash.
And if you don't heed the prophet and the brass,
I'm gonna have to put a fuckin bullet in your ass.

Crack will loot your life and make your souls dark and hollow,
So keep your mind and body clean and yo ass will follow.
And when the curtain drops and the show is over,
You get to keep it all in eternal fields of clover.

Church Sells Main Street To Saudis

Facing mounting pressure from local activists, as well as litigation from the American Civil Liberties Union, the LDS Church announced today it has sold the disputed Main Street Plaza to Saudi Arabia.

The several-block stretch of property on Main Street, recently purchased by the church from the City of Salt Lake for $3 million, was also the subject of growing controversy.

According to sources close to the transaction, the LDS Church and the Kingdom of Saudi Arabia have entered into an agreement late Saturday evening as the Muslim Holy period of Ramadhan was winding down. The selling price was disclosed at $103 million thereby netting the church a $100 million windfall profit for its one-year investment in the property.

The development of the Main Street Plaza has been under public scrutiny since the church first undertook measures to obtain the property. During a City Council meeting in June, 1998, church officials appeased council members by promising to develop the Main Street property into a park where the public could experience "a little bit of Paris."

However, the plan to redevelop the property came under fire when church officials acquired the property and afterwards announced that it would establish and enforce certain behavioral 'guidelines for public safety' for access to the park such as prohibitions on radios, tattoos, body-piercings, tobacco use, and public speaking.

The ACLU immediately filed suit against the city claiming the sale was unconstitutional and that in effect the transaction was depriving citizens of public property protected by the Articles of the United States Constitution that permit free speech, access, and the right to assemble.

ACLU attorney Gloria Weinstein said, "The church's vision of a little bit of Paris seems hauntingly similar to the Nazi's vision of Paris during their occupation of France in World War II. What we have here is the creation of an ecclesiastical ghetto where jack-boot, white-shirted missionaries would patrol the grounds removing anyone that did not comply with the church's 'guidelines for public safety.'"

However, today's decision to sell Main Street to Saudi Arabia left even the harshest critics of the church dumbfounded.

In a hastily arranged news conference, Church Spokesman Dale Bills said, "The decision by church authorities to sell the Main Street Plaza is not necessarily a capitulation to legal and political pressures."

When asked why the church had decided to sell the property, Bills replied, "The church has a duty to be a good steward in its role as both citizen and public servant. We felt it was in the public's interest to expand their view and experience of foreign cultures such as the Kingdom of Saudi Arabia, which has strikingly similar tenets as our own faith.

Muslims are a lot like the saints. We have kingdoms and they have kingdoms. We wear traditional garments and they do too. We do not consume alcohol and neither do they. And their views on women and polygamy are certainly not unfamiliar to us."

Spokesman for King Fahd bin Abdul Aziz of Saudi Arabia released a press statement this afternoon "King Fahd wishes to convey his gratitude to the American people and the Jesus Christ Church of Latter-day Saints. We welcome this historic moment as an opportunity to bridge the gap between our cultures. We want to assure the citizens of Salt Lake City we will carry forward the original plans by the LDS Church for redevelopment of the plaza. The guidelines for public safety as put forth by the LDS Church will remain the same. However, we feel it is fair to advise the public that the penalties for failure to comply with the guidelines will be somewhat different than what they are accustomed to. The penalties for guideline violations will be more in accordance with Islamic law. Violators will be subject to stoning, amputations of extremities, and beheading."

LDS Church Spokesman Bills said, "I'd like to see the ACLU organize their first demonstration on the grounds of Main Street Plaza now. Those Muslims are all business. Let 'em take those Arabs to court. They're going to get a little bit of Riyadh. The streets are going to be littered with limbs, torsos, and heads. Heck, I heard they are going to build a cave to detain menstruating women. Those liberals at the ACLU are going to long for the halcyon days when we ran the plaza."

Bills added, "With the proceeds from this sale, the church plans to acquire Bally's Casino in Las Vegas. We are going to let the citizens of Las Vegas experience a little bit of Salt Lake City."

Porn Czar Arrested for Miscegenation

In a "bizarre" twist, the nation's first statewide Porn Czar (Utah's only 40-year-old Mormon virgin), Paula Houston, was charged with one felony count of unlawful miscegenation with barnyard animals late Saturday evening.

Utah, the country's notorious fledgling theocracy, has tried unsuccessfully to legislate morality and drawn the attention of news and law enforcement agencies worldwide. The state recently appointed a devout Mormon virgin, a woman who professes to have never seen a penis and whose religious tenets prohibit the placing of genitalia in one's mouth for gratification, to head up statewide law enforcement on smut.

Acting on an anonymous tip, police invaded the barn of Hyrum Jensen in Springville, UT where they discovered Utah's Porn Czar, Mz. Houston, sleeping with one of Mr. Jensen's pigs.

Mz. Houston stood speechless as law enforcement officials took photographs and collected evidence from the scene, which included what was believed to be remnants of Mz. Houston's ruptured hymen as well as pig ejaculate.

Houston was recently appointed to seek out pornography and obscenity in Utah and to assist legislators in re-writing pornography statutes. However, Houston's appointment to the post drew criticism from all sides of law enforcement, the ACLU, The NAACP, The Utah Bar, as well as several retarded people who all questioned Houston's qualifications for the position. Apparently everyone but Utah Attorney General Mark Shurtleff considered Houston completely unqualified for the position due to Houston's lack of sexual experience, knowledge, and "exposure." Accusations turned ugly as those opposed to the appointment accused Houston of being a lesbian.

Houston, a 40-year-old self-professed "virgin" denied rumors she was a lesbian and insisted that she has maintained her celibacy in observance of her Mormon beliefs. Said Houston, "Janet Reno has never been married and I fail to see how anyone can infer either Reno or myself, both who have law enforcement positions, are lesbians simply because we are professionals that happen to look like diesel mechanics."

In December, 1999 Houston stated, "Although I have never had sex nor watched any sexual acts performed on video, I know obscenity and pornography when I see it."

Shortly afterward, Houston began an unprecedented campaign to get local officials in Utah to ban all literature written by Henry Miller, Oscar Wilde, Walt Whitman, and Theodore Dreiser.

Soon after her appointment, Houston forced the Salt Lake County Attorney's office to indict a man under Utah's pornography statutes for publishing his account of an incident that took place in the New Mexico desert. Steve Benson and a companion were traveling on Route 66 when Mr. Benson's passenger felt the urge to urinate. Mr. Benson pulled his automobile on the side of the road where both men exposed their genitalia and urinated on a cluster of rocks. A rattlesnake that was nesting beneath the rocks rose up from its hiding place and bit Mr. Benson's passenger on the penis, injecting the victim with a lethal dose of venom. Remembering his Boy Scout training, Mr. Benson took out his pocketknife and made a small x-shaped incision above the fang marks on his companion's penis and immediately began sucking out the venom from the penis. His passenger survived the snake attack and was treated at a local hospital.

Benson published his heroic account in the Arizona Republic and was later indicted after Utah Troopers pulled Mr. Benson over on I-15 for suspicion of trafficking beer and a discovered copy of the pornographic newspaper account of the snakebite incident in Mr. Benson's trunk.

Houston also hopes to pursue a criminal indictment against the University of Utah for forcing theater students to say "fuck" and "god-dammit" during performances. Said Houston; "This is salacious and gratuitous material and it is patently offensive under any community standard anywhere in the United States."

Houston circulated petitions within numerous communities to get referendums on local ballots to outlaw the words: "shit, fuck, motherfucker, cock, cocksucker, twat, prick, and Democrat."

With respect to her arrest, Houston denied any personal involvement with her porcine suitor and brushed off accusations saying, "When it is part of your job, I don't see it as against your religion. Somebody has to deal with it, even if it's not the most pleasant thing in the world. Besides, after I came, I made him stop and light me a cigarette. But being the pig that he is, he wiped his dick on the curtains and fell asleep. I feel so violated. Sex is totally overrated."

Andy Baillargeon

Ask Al

Mr. Al Koholic is a licensed drunk, and has many years of alcohol counseling experience. Al has been serving the public for over 20 years and he's finally come to Utah. If you have any liquor-related questions or anything intoxicating on your mind, write to Al at free@wildutah.net. Dear Abby has nothing on this guy.

Dear Al,

I recently hit it big out on the town. As I proceeded to get shit-faced, the inevitable beer-goggle phenomenon took hold and the snaggle-toothed girl in the corner was starting to look damn fine. I started talking to her and after a few more gin and tonics and a dance, I took her home. The next morning I awoke as if it were a bad dream, only to find Princess Bucktooth lying next to me, buck-naked. Why does this phenomenon occur, and what can I do to avoid another such encounter?

Sincerely, Leg Chewed-off Coyote

Dear Mr. Coyote,

You may think this only happens to men; but on the contrary, small amounts of alcohol in women produce testosterone and an increased libido. A man's sex drive will actually start to decrease with consumption, but a man's decreased sex drive is still much higher than a woman's increased sex drive. This is called the "Men Are Pigs" theory. When you consume alcohol, your judgement is impaired and the alcohol disables the brain centers that inhibit your behavior. To avoid these undesirable situations, simply stop drinking; but since I know that'll never happen, next time bring a buddy you trust to be your voice of reason, should you find another girl in the corner. Otherwise you're pretty much S.O.L. I believe beer goggles are the Universe's way of giving everyone the chance to get some lovin'. As they say, everyone needs a little lovin' sometimes.

Dear Al,

My friend Damian distills cayenne pepper in alcohol, and packages it in a one ounce vile. The stuff makes me feel great, but I was wondering if it's illegal for him to sell this since there is a fair amount of alcohol in it.

Heat Fiend

Dear Mr. Heat,

This is a tough one, but yes, he can sell these little gems as long as the intent is to use it as a spice or additive, much like a hot sauce. This type of product is called a tincture; that is a substance held in alcoholic menstruum. I'm familiar with this pepper and I can say if anyone plans on using this in heavy doses, say your prayers. I once took a swig in the name of experience, (and maybe a quick hot buzz) and what little I remember was a trip to the depths of hell. When it finally gets through the system, I can tell you it's twice as hot upon exit. So tell your friend to keep the stuff coming, and put me down for two bottles.

Dear Al,

In my church, it is considered a sin to drink alcohol. I have never tried alcohol in fear of eternal damnation, but I'm very curious about the whole thing. What does it taste like, what does being drunk feel like, will I go to hell for drinking?

Please respond soon

Going to hell? You must be LIVING in hell. What the hell do those church people know about hell anyway except for the fact that most of them will get well acquainted with hell in their afterlife? In fact, the early Church declared alcohol as an inherently good gift from God to be used and enjoyed. Jesus himself drank and approved of its moderate consumption. So to hell with those church people, find you a cold one, bottoms up and enjoy. To answer your questions about taste and the drunken sensation, it tastes like shit but the sensation feels great. My suggestion is to take it slow, start with a wine cooler, which will break you into the taste with minimal drunken effect. Work gradually into the harder stuff, and remember, public intoxication can be dangerous for a rookie. In the meantime, eat, drink and be merry. And if you think a drink sends you to hell, then heaven is going to be a lonely

150

place.

Dear Al K.,

O.K., so I've been noticing how whenever my Psychology professor starts lecturing, I feel that I understand less and less what he is talking about. My friends and I have been throwing back the beer much harder lately and I heard that drinking beer can kill brain cells and make you dumber. Is the beer thing true, or do ya think it might be something else.

Thanks

Missing something

Dear Missing,

Actually no, moderate consumption of alcohol does not kill brain cells; it actually helps with the cognitive process. In fact, I'm drinking right now. I always have a drink when I read your letters. You say you've been drinking a lot more lately, and in this case, yes, it does kill brain cells, but only the weak ones. So here again you're getting smarter. That's the scientific view, now lets get down to the real issue. First of all, do you remember why you took Psychology? I remember why I did. Psych class is where all the chicks hang out. How can you possibly concentrate with all the mini skirts and tank tops? Don't fret this one; befriend one of these skirts and set-up a few study sessions. You'll kill two birds, get a date and pass your class. Oh yeah, keep drinking; it can only help.

BYU vs. MTV

The world of "cool" that watches MTV sits amazed at a sheltered girl who knows nothing about the "Real World."

Many of you may have already heard about the poor little girl who was booted from BYU for cohabiting on the MTV series "The Real World." When every BYU student registers, they are expected to follow the honor code of the University. One of these codes involves residential-living requirements. Students of the opposite sex are only allowed to be in the lobby and kitchen areas of the dorm. The bedroom and bathroom areas are strictly prohibited. In an off-campus situation, members of the opposite sex are only allowed in the living room and kitchen. We want to know what happens when the opposing gender needs to use the can.

BYU has recently taken issue with one of its most famous students (not Steve Young) regarding these residential living honor codes. Julie from the New Orleans "Real World" was suspended from BYU for breaking this honor code. By joining the show, Julie had to live with six people she had never met—four of them were boys. These other six people were quite diverse; two black kids (one of them a boy), a gay boy, and two hip white kids (one was a boy).

As you might have imagined, Julie's childhood was a sheltered one. She was born in Provo, and raised Mormon in Delafield, Wisconsin. The Real World's melting pot of cast-members was intrigued and confused by our young hero. When she would use the word "colored" to refer to blacks, the other members of the show would gasp in concern. They harassed her about not knowing "common, American knowledge," but tried to understand her innocence.

Julie was fascinated with the gay boy's lifestyle because it was so foreign to her. Julie was actually getting a taste of the real world.

Oh my heck, what had Julie done? She was breaking every rule she was taught growing up, and discovering a life of her own. Shame on her!

Julie's devotion to her religion is still strong, and yet she wants to forge ahead and open her mind to new ideas and beliefs. Julie is a pioneer, and actually, she even has a great sense of humor (something lacking in Utah's real world). When she was asked who she told first about being on the show, she said she didn't tell anyone for two days.

"The hardest person to tell was my dad because he had made me promise I wouldn't do it if I got picked. I broke it to him really easy. I said, 'Dad, I'm pregnant. Wait, no… I'm actually just living in Sin City on The Real World.'"

Julie has guts to ignore some of her religious beliefs in order to learn about the world. We hope there are a few more out there like her.

"Real World Julie" is Wild Utah's hero of the week.

Pioneer Day Fun

Well, the coveted July 24th Pioneer Day has come and gone, but the memory still lingers. This is a special day where Utahans celebrate the rise of a state and a legacy. Many Utah folks spend a nice day at the parade followed by barbecue fun with family and friends. Since we here at Wild Utah aren't "many" folks, we decided to celebrate a little differently.

10 p.m. the night before: Warmed up the liver with a few drinks at the bar. Also slammed some shots for good measure.

10:45: Remembered that tomorrow was a day off and proceeded to get shit-faced.

12:15 a.m.: Scrounged up last of change to purchase the last-call beer. Found several attractive ladies and invited them back for an after-hours hot tub party.

12:16: Turned down by attractive ladies, chugged beer, invited ugly ones and stumbled home in mass.

Pioneer Day 1 p.m.: Awake in a haze but still somewhat refreshed. Realize not alone in bed; chew arm off.

1:05: Fix a screwdriver with remaining arm to lift the haze and thank the lord that we remembered to purchase liquor goods the day before.

1:15: Repeat the above step until haze is gone and shove ugly chick out of the door. Should wave, but scratch groin region with remaining arm.

2:35: By this time, a new cloud of haze is forming; remember we were having a party for the big day.

3:00: Think about straightening up the house, but crack a beer instead and proceed to wander around town recruiting partygoers.

10:10: First guests arrive and the carnage begins.

10:35: A group of 10 young ladies arrives and any previous fears of a Sausage-Fest fade away into the night.

11:00: Line up multiple shots of Tequila and Bacardi, slam and repeat until everyone forgets their own name.

11:45 and 12:30: Cops arrive, as expected, with noise complaint and roommate almost goes to jail for mouthing off.

1:15 a.m.: Party starts thinning out and several couples retreat for some premarital activity. The less fortunate continue to binge drink and decide some gambling would be a good idea.

3:00: All debts get paid and the party disperses.

3:00 p.m. next day: Wake up with clothes and shoes on and realize we all missed work. Oh well, might as well crack a beer.

Pioneer Day is a special day in Utah history with good wholesome fun had by all. See ya next year.

152

The True American Legend

The true American legend has intrigued the public since the early part of the century. We marvel at the original classic machines and the image they have come to portray. This is the legend of Harley Davidson.

Harley symbolizes freedom. But for many people, Harley represents an outlaw renegade lifestyle. How did this image of the rough and tumble outlaw come about? Well, after the Second World War, outcast veterans found life back in the States overwhelmingly dull compared to the combat zones in Europe. These vets embraced a wild life, and did so with the help of their Harley Davidsons.

"Wino" Willie Forkner joined these souls together and formed one of the first motorcycle clubs in history, "The Boozefighters" (BFMC). The group pushed the limits of their Hog's and themselves, racing to extreme speeds and pushing the danger envelope. As the group's name suggests, you can be sure there was no lack of the forbidden fruits of hops, barley, and wine. This combination of speed and liquor helped the Boozefighters obtain a less than desirable reputation with the common folk.

The media took that reputation to the next level when the BFMC attended the infamous Hollister, CA Fourth of July party of 1947. The party got out of hand and a police car was destroyed—among other things. The tabloids unjustly placed the blame squarely on the shoulders of the BFMC; and thus was born the outlaw biker image or the "One-percenters." Not one BFMC member was involved in the destruction, but the image was set and the world was seduced by the outlaw biker.

The "One-percenters" term was coined because it is said that outlaw bikers represent one percent of all bike owners. The most renowned of this group is, of course, the Hell's Angels (HA's). They own chapters around the country and they keep a discrete profile for obvious reasons. You may run into a HA or even another outlaw group in your life. Confrontation is highly discouraged (again for obvious reasons). Outlaw groups are just out for a good time along with the rest of the 99-percenters. Trouble starts with a drunken aggressor who thinks it would be cool to start shit with one. But this guy will only find an early grave.

Despite the dark perception, the Harley Davidson still continues to intrigue the masses. The waiting list for a factory Hog is an easy two years. Buying a used one could mean a cross-country trip and a healthy pocket book.

Has this intrigue been fueled for almost a century by Harley's renegade image alone? No way. You can feel the deep crack of the pipes when you kick over the mill, and all your worries are drowned out by the wind chapping your face. What else could you possibly need?

Those of you who have had the pleasure can relate; but for you other poor saps, put this on your "things to do before you die," list. And when you finally come to your senses, add going to a biker rally to that list. You have a few options: the Fourth of July extravaganza in Humbolt, Iowa; Daytona Bike Week in Florida; or the granddaddy of em' all, The Black Hills Classic in Sturgis, South Dakota. Any of these will do if you're looking to unleash the Harley man or biker mama in you.

Sturgis is the once in a lifetime experience that happens once a year. You will enjoy a myriad of live bands and parties 'till he sun comes up. Don't miss out on the biker rodeo events. This may be your only chance to see bikini clad women bite a wiener hanging from a string off the back of a moving motorcycle, or watch guys push the limits in the "how slow can you ride without touching the ground" competition. Finally, if you attend Sturgis this year, you will be treated to the world's largest biker bar, "Full Throttle Saloon."

The legacy of the Harley Davidson is a strong one. It has evolved from the first motorized bicycle to a Knucklehead, Panhead, Shovelhead, Evolution, Twin-Cam, and finally the new V-Rod. We have watched the Harley turn from a bike to a way of life. The Harley image has taken its fair share of blows, but through it all, the Harley Davidson Motorcycle is, and always will be, the most popular bike in the world—and the True American Legend.

Rock Oakeson

"Reparative Therapy" at BYU in 1972

In the August 2000 issue of The Pillar, an excellent article appeared about the dangers of so-called "ex-gay" Christian ministries and associated "reparative therapy." It is fascinating to me that such things are ubiquitously spoken of these days, because back when I was a college student, nobody had heard of such a phenomenon. I think I ended up unwittingly being one of the ground-breakers, so to speak, in 1972. I actually had the audacity to ask for such a therapy while a student at Brigham Young University.

I was quite confused at that point in my life. I knew without any doubt that I was gay, but I had no friends or acquaintances who were out—no positive reference points at all. So the only thing I heard was how sinful it was from my church leaders, and how contemptuous it was from all the derisive guys in my dormitory. I had spent a lifetime up until then not fitting in very well with society in general and the LDS Church in particular; so it was important to me to find out how to conform at all costs. Gaining acceptance from family and friends was an obsession by the time I got to BYU. So after years of torturing myself thinking of how to "fix" all this, I decided to tell my BYU Branch President.

In retrospect, I recall how embarrassed everybody involved was to proceed with my request. They complimented me on my desire to "leave the muck and mire," and go through "proper repentance channels;" but I could tell they were in a major quandary. They were duty-bound and had to do something to follow through.

Eventually my Branch President said that he spoke with a psychologist over in the Smoot Building's Counseling Center who would see me twice a week. He mentioned that this was a free service offered to full-time BYU students. I figured this could only help me, but was even happier that it was free. I asked if this would remain totally confidential, and he said that it would be just between himself, the psychologist, and me. I found that acceptable. After all, these were the proper channels, weren't they?

During the first visit to this psychologist, I had no idea how to proceed except to tell him everything that was going on with me at school and in the dorm. I was very honest. I let him in on the fact that, just in this semester alone, I had three gay professors (even an idiot could tell, I thought, but my own gaydar never lied); I had a crush on seven of the 40 guys on my floor in Deseret Towers; I had heard 27 derogatory comments about gays and lesbians the past week; and I couldn't stand my homophobic roommate.

Plus, I told him how an older person, unknown to me, had called me wanting an "interview" earlier that week. This person claimed to be a member of my stake presidency, so not wanting to be disobedient, I went to his Harris Fine Arts Center office to talk with him. It turned out that he had been let in on our little secret which I thought only included my

Branch President and this counselor. This member of my stake presidency had asked me if I was repenting. I said yes. He asked me if I had ever had any sexual experience with anybody at BYU. I said no, and told him I was a still a virgin. He asked me if I knew anybody at BYU who was having homosexual feelings. I told him that I didn't discuss sexual feelings with anybody, and that he would have to ask people for himself—it was none of my business. It looked like what turned into the infamous gay "witch hunt" at BYU had already begun.

My psychologist told me that he had told nobody, so it must have been my Branch President. But I wasn't too upset about it, because the proper channels were the proper channels. I really wanted to give reparative therapy my best shot so that in the future, should I remain as I always had been, nobody could honestly tell me I didn't try.

After spending two semesters with this same psychologist and getting nowhere talking about everyone from my parents and family, to my friends and teachers, he eventually decided to get another staff psychologist to chat with me and see if anything else could be done. I must commend the first one for his open-mindedness and zeal to try to help me, because this second one seemed very annoyed with me and detached. Not even making much eye contact with me, he decided after four sessions that hypnosis was the answer. I was actually very excited, that late Spring day, to go to his office to be hypnotized.

Thinking that this might be the answer, I gladly relaxed as I lay on his sofa and did everything he told me. Basically it amounted to staring at a small statue of Charlie Chaplin while he told me in a low voice that I had genitals, that I was able to use them normally, and that from now on I would. After this 10-minute session, I obviously felt no different, nor did I continue to think that these inspired men of the Mormon counseling world knew what they were doing. I very honestly explained to this second therapist that I would rather return to the first. He seemed relieved.

I went back to my first therapist, no longer having much faith in this process, but still willing to do whatever he prescribed. He thought that we had talked through things enough, and now felt like bio-feedback was the answer. So twice a week for the rest of the Summer, I went to his office, took a few clothes off, let him attach cold, gel-coated diodes to various parts of my body while he monitored the way I relaxed. He and I learned two things from this: that I could relax deeply when I wanted to, and that bio-feedback had absolutely nothing to do with changing a person's sexual orientation.

At the end of his rope, he finally disclosed a "failure-proof action" that we could take that he said he had been saving. He asked if it would be acceptable to me to call in my entire branch presidency one day and, in his office, have them anoint me with oil and give me a blessing to cast out any homosexual demons that might be lurking somewhere inside my body and soul. I remember mockingly asking him if this was the definition of "the last straw." He smiled apologetically and said, "I guess so."

So we made an appointment for when my Branch President, his two counselors, the psychologist and I could meet there, and we met. It was a late evening, and all of them stood around me in the circle as they poured olive oil on my head, laid their hands over my oily scalp, and with the maudlin and overly sanctimonious tones of my Branch President's voice, cast out "in the name of Jesus" any "unclean spirits" that were causing or aiding my "lack of feelings for women and abnormal desires for men."

I remember the moment it was over; I stood on cue to shake all their hands. No change. Nothing. I felt no different at all. But as I walked back to the dormitory that evening, a strange kind of freedom came over me—a freedom in knowing that I was who I was, through no choice or fault of my own, and that I couldn't change even if somebody else thought I should. Nor did I need to be forgiven.

I wish I could say that I came out of the closet that night feeling free of all guilt and shame, but I can't. I may have learned that I couldn't change my feelings, but I still tried hiding them for another 15 years. After a two-year mission to Sapporo, Japan, then serving the church in many capacities, and finally even attempting a temple marriage, I learned more than ever before that I am who I am. I stopped worrying about whether or not people accepted me. I finally began to accept myself—the real purpose of life.

Living in Orange County, California, in 1987 at the age of 33, I had my marriage annulled, came out of the closet, left Mormonism and started getting involved in the gay community there. Even now, my many friends and loved ones, along with my partner of 3 fi years, have given me nothing but support. Life is open and guilt-free now that I have learned what few people have from direct experience. I will never forget my year in "reparative" therapy. Even though it has become a hot topic these days, with the therapy itself no doubt more formalized than mine, I still can't imagine that its essence has changed much—or become any more successful—than mine was back in 1972.

If It Itches, Scratch It!

We've all had them. Very embarrassing experiences. I'm talking VERY embarrassing ones. They're the ones we don't tell even our best friend.

But I have learned that being completely open and honest about everything is the best therapy in the universe. I think we should all come out of every closet and let the world see us as we really are. When you give no power to the opinions and judgments of others, they can't hurt you. I've watched judgmental people, groups, and even large organizations become absolutely impotent to affect me—all because I have nothing to hide and am joyful and proud of who and what I am.

So, in keeping with my own therapeutic advice, I would like to share my most embarrassing moment with all of you. (Exciting, isn't it?)

Although a Jew by birth, I was adopted into a Mormon family very early on and raised that way. So after a couple years at Brigham Young University, I felt compelled to serve a two-year mission for the church. They sent me to Hawaii to learn Japanese (Provo's "Mission Training Center" was not built yet), then on to Sapporo, Japan.

Both Hawaii and Japan were the two most humid places I had ever lived, and as humiliating as it was in front of all the other Elders in our mission, I started getting "jock rash." And

boy, did I get it bad! It started in the usual area, then spread up onto my chest and down my legs! For almost three linear feet, I was red and oozy, up and down the front of my body.

I tell you this by way of background information. I haven't gotten to the really embarrassing part yet.

When I returned home after the two years, I was still affected and reeling from my itchy/scratchy affair. And I eventually returned to BYU to finish my last semesters before receiving my Bachelor of Music degree. While there, even though I applied stinging/burning medicine on myself every morning and evening, I often could not endure any longer the itchy agony I was going through. So naturally, when nobody was looking, I just had to scratch violently in places only Homer Simpson or Al Bundy wouldn't be discrete about. (I usually sat at the back of classrooms)

The awful rash was slowly going away millimeter by millimeter by the end of my first semester back from Japan. But one day it was itchier than usual. I was on the fifth floor of BYU's main library in the center of campus (this floor was the "Music Library"). As I stood alone in the aisles of the stacks of music scores (at least, I thought I was alone), I just had to unfasten my belt, unzip my zipper, pull my pants down to half mast and insert both hands into the front and back of my temple garments—and let my fingernails go to work.

You can't possibly imagine how pleasant it can be to scratch such an intense itch, especially over such a large area in that region of your body. I'm sure the look on my face reflected this tactile, celestial ecstasy. I think my eyes had even rolled to the back of my head.

Can you picture this? I mean, I was going at it for at least a good minute, and looking every bit as blissed-out as imaginable. Suddenly, right in the middle of this sensory nirvana, I heard a familiar voice that pretty much electrocuted me back to reality:

"What an interesting activity, Rock," it said. "This isn't something I'd do in a public place, if I were you."

Shit! It was my "Theory of Baroque Counterpoint" professor! My face must have turned redder than my crotch as I realized that, with everything hanging out the way it was (if you catch my drift), he would now know that I was Jewish. His facial expression has been indelibly etched into my mind: total disdain mixed with abject horror, kind of like what you would expect from an Amish man trapped inside a light bulb factory.

I quickly organized my parts, tucked my shirt into my trousers, zipped and buckled. When I looked up again, I couldn't believe that he was still there staring! Only now the look on his face was as if one of those light bulbs had just turned on over his head. Apparently he just realized (or verified) something, then turned and quickly walked toward the Men's room.

Well, there you have it. Thank you for letting me share. Now go thou and do likewise with your own experiences. You'll feel much better. As for my professor, all I can say is that he seemed so much happier the rest of the semester, walking with a definite lilt and speaking with a cadence he had not allowed himself before. Oh, by the way, I got an "A" in my counterpoint class. Don't ask me why.

Babbage

Screw the Luddites

I just saw a demo of the new Sony Aibo/2. That's right—your dog, version 2. It's kind of scary that we're kicking off the consumer robotic revolution with a fake dog, but I think they picked the right household pet. If you accept the fact that if your little cat weighed a 100 pounds more, it would kill you and eat you, you can begin to see why a nation beset by Godzilla for the last 50-plus years would focus on a mechanical Rover.

It's a pretty psycho version 2. The old model could look cute, roll around, sit, and respond to some basic commands—as long as the TV, stereo, and children were all turned off. The new one, wow! You can shove an 802.11b card up its backside and this puppy can read you e-mail! How freaky is that? I had an inanimate object talk to me in college once. It was a stuffed toy that cost about 20 bucks; the animating "substance" cost under $20... considerably less than the two grand the new Aibo unit sets you back.

Even more amazing, this puppy sports a built in video camera you can control from your PC. You heard that right; you can DRIVE this puppy. You can control him/her remotely around the house and check things out. It works up to 150 feet (more if you have a good antenna on your base station). Once you start thinking about it, the potential for mischief increases exponentially. Proof that the folks at Sony are just as perverted as the rest of us—it beeps in remote mode and it can't look up more than 45 degrees. The fortune you were going to make through www.upskirtspics.com will have to wait.

I have this Bob Newhart sketch in my head I can't get rid of. It's the one where Columbus is trying to sell tobacco to the King of Spain. It got me thinking about how you sell a $2000, e-mail reading, spy poochie. I imagine the following conversation is coming soon to an electronic pet store near you:

"So it can read my e-mail?"

"Oh yes, right off the Internet. You point it at your e-mail account and it will let you know when you have mail and read it back to you. It's like those talking robots at Disney."

"Really? How does it do it?"

"It has a wireless network card in its ass. It connects to the Internet and picks up your e-mail using the ass-card and some software."

"So for two grand I get a dog that connects to the Internet through its ass?"

"That's right. You can even drive it around the house and see what's happening." "Thanks to the card in its ass?"

"That's right! You've read that the 802.11b standard would revolutionize networking. Here it is in action. This puppy has an Ethernet connection in its ass."

"And it will read my mail?"

"Oh yes, and fetch, follow commands, beg, act cute— the whole thing."

"All thanks to that 802 whatever card?"

"Nearly, it does cute things without the card; you need the card to connect to the Internet."

"What happens if I just buy the card and shove that up my current dogs ass?"

To quote Accenture, "Now it starts getting interesting."

Screw the Luddites II

Most of us have heard about the James Bond film "The Spy who loved me." I have a new little wonder in my house I like to call 'The Spy I love.' Unlike James Bond, I'm not a usually early adopter. I like other people to make sure the ejector seat/nuclear propelled ski poles work before I buy.

This year things have been a little different. I broke my early adopter rule and bought a Tivo. I read all the reviews; I looked at Replay; I considered waiting for the "it-will-even-cure-cancer" X-Box, and finally gave in.

Some things about Tivo are truly fantastic—there is always something good on my TV now. Some things are truly terrifying—my Tivo is a Bondian nightmare that calls the nemesis every night to report on my viewing activities. What's worse? It does this no matter how many times I save its life or compliment it on its svelte body.

The literature swears they collect anonymous view habits . . . they say Tivo uses an advanced keyword search for the recommendations . . . but come on. After a couple weeks, this machine started to suggest I watch LEXX. Could this be because it deduced from my viewing habits? At first I thought not, then after careful consideration I thought again. I like Star Trek; I also like girls in bikinis, the Man Show & Baywatch (with the sound off, of course). I also watch the Discovery Channel, Tech TV, movies, PBS specials, etc. But this machine honed right in and said, "You may talk Discovery Channel, but I know you simply dig chicks and SciFi!" I figure a Cleopatra 2525 recommendation is just around the corner.

As for LEXX—it's Sex and Scifi—if you like that kind of thing take a gander... The Spy I love called it, and I'll be watching it again.

This darling bundle of joy reads my mind all the time. It records what I tell it to whenever it's on. I can say "DON'T EVER MISS ANYTHING WITH CARRIE ANNE MOSS," and it won't. This is how I discovered my leather clad Matrix babe actually started in a show called Models, Inc. that makes Melrose place look like a period drama—but more on that another time. I can tell my Tivo to catch whatever game I want. Thus I am guaranteed a vivid disappointment every season when I tell it to never miss a Red Sox game.

These pieces of magic pale in comparison to my favorite feature. "DON'T EVER MAKE ME WATCH AN AD AGAIN." This simple phrase is why this spy will never leave my house. I've stopped watching ads completely. Forget "Pause Live TV." I don't know a single owner who watches Live TV anymore. It's far too frustrating. But once you've saved seven minutes of ads for every 30 in front of the box, you will never go back!

So there you have it. "Don't ever make me watch an ad again." This is the catchphrase they were too afraid to tell you. But that's why we Tivo-users love this baby. So go and buy one. Accept the fact that it will know your inner desires intimately. Accept the fact that it will hand them off to marketers. Accept the fact that it will report every time you watch Baywatch and Discovery. Because every time you hit fast-forward passed those ads it will feel worth it!

Contributors

Ski Utah With A Hangover

by Garth Schwellenbach

3 a.m.: I stumbled into my apartment, thinking about sleep after a night of band practice. When band practice lasts until 3 a.m., not one of us is sober. As I staggered through my front door I saw on the counter in front of me a Tupperware container full of Rocky Road Ice Cream Toppin (a brainchild of my roommate) and a small note: "Call Tommy when you get in, he wants you to go on the Interconnect Tour tomorrow." To this I chuckled, and decided 3 a.m. was not the best time to call Tommy, and early was not the best time for me to wake up in the morning. I told myself that if for some reason he calls in the morning, and for some even stranger reason I wake up when I hear the phone, there might be a wee possibility I get up and think about going.

7:30 a.m.: I awoke to the phone. The answering machine plays, "When you get up and figure out what your doing today, call me if you want to go on the Interconnect Tour." If I was in any shape to laugh at this point I would have, but instead I had that feeling you get when you drank far too many 3.2 beers the night before. I was weak and shaky, I needed to piss, I needed some water, I needed more sleep. After making water, and drinking water, I climbed back in bed and tried to sleep. I couldn't do it—it was gone; I started to have those thoughts that maybe some nice snow was out

there, and once that thought gets started, sleep is no more. I got out of bed and went to the phone to make the call. I found I had a half-hour to get my shit together, and be at the resort center Jans. I proceeded to tear through my room desperately trying to remember what it was I needed to go skiing. There are lots of things to remember.

I somehow got out of the house and in the car with enough time to stop at the King for a tasty sausage egg biscuit (the grease was needed) and got to Jans with time to spare. I was feeling good, and maybe even looking good; the lack of sleep and abundance of alcohol in my system had not yet kicked in. The guides showed up a few minutes later, and we proceeded with the usual form filling and introductions. It was a small group: me, one other journalist (I'm not really a journalist, but I can pretend), and three guides. Not a bad ratio. Two of the guides, Steve Schueler and Rodd Keller, skied with us; and the other, John Hughes, drove the shuttle and got a few runs in on his own.

The Interconnect Tour, which is run by Ski Utah, has been around for eighteen years, so it isn't some unorganized, run-out-of-the-trunk-of-a-car kind of deal. They know what's going on, and how to do what they do. The guides have broad backgrounds in skiing and snow safety, which is a serious issue in the Wasatch. They even look professional in their red Fila jackets with "Ski Utah" on the back, and all donning K2 skis (with pins of course).

After strapping on our avalanche beacons and getting the

safety talk, we headed up the Payday lift at PCMR—the first of five mountains that we would ski that day. We worked our way to Jupiter, and out of bounds at the patrol shack. Dropping into Big Cottonwood Canyon wasn't the best snow in the world, no thanks to the scouring winds that had blown in the few days prior.

After a quick ski we ended up at our second resort, Solitude. From Solitude we went straight to number three, Brighton where our ever-knowledgeable guides found us some creamy snow in the trees. The fog in my head was finally lifting, and we headed back to Solitude for lunch. After a juicy cheeseburger, we headed back up the lift, on our way to Little Cottonwood Canyon.

I've skied a lot in the Wasatch, both at resorts and touring, but I was still amazed at the proximity of the resorts. I knew they were all close, but I figured we would have to use skins and do a little hiking. There were some run-outs and traverses where we did a little pushing and skating, but no actual hiking was necessary. That said, if the whole group wants to hike, it is an option. Being a small group, we opted for one quick hike to better our turns. I was still trying to clean out my system from the night before.

On our way to Alta we found some decent turns in the Grizzly Gulch area, thanks to the terrain knowledge of our guides. From Alta we made it over to the fifth and final resort of the day, Snowbird. There we took the last tram up, and got in some surprisingly good turns as the sun finally came out to end the day. John was waiting for us with the van and we piled in for the return trip to Park City.

It is now 6:30 p.m., and I'm tired; it was an unexpectedly long day, but it was all very well worth it. The Interconnect Tour is a great way to get out and away from the resorts and see some terrain and views that most people don't get. When I left in the morning I didn't know what to expect: hard-core touring, easy resort skiing, both? It ended up being resort skiing with some backcountry turns, without the work. This was a good thing for the state my mind and body was in, and would be a good thing for a flatlander. Although maybe not the most challenging day for a seasoned ski tourer, the Interconnect Tour is a great day for a skier without much backcountry experience, looking for more adventure than a resort can offer.

The Tour offers views and turns that are unreachable at any resort, as well as the bragging rights of skiing five resorts in the same day without driving. Now I have to go to another band practice. It sometimes hurts, but it's always a good hurt.

The Rosemont

by Robert E. Beer

In 1972, or thereabouts, I took my longhaired, pseudo-psycho weirdness and moved to Hutchinson, Kansas after I got laid off from the Guerdon Trailer factory in nearby Newton.

My brother Jim was living there and said I could get a job at the construction site he worked at, where they were building the new bank downtown. I moved into a wino flophouse, The Rosemont; Jim had a cheap room there also.

The joint was run by Ruby, a sexually frustrated, dried-up old hide who made it her business to know everyone else's. She was a prune-faced, faded pink threadworn-robe-wearing closet-wino herself, with a wrinkled nose, curler-infested, patchy hair and a well-earned sour apple constitution. She made the Wicked Witch of the West look downright hospitable. But no one really cared, as long as they could go to their room and drink the cheap wine until they either puked or passed out; all was well in Ruby's world. The only thing she wouldn't approve of was visitors, especially those of the opposite sex.

At my new job, I was what was euphemistically referred to as a "construction laborer," which meant I swept up the newly built floors' attendant sawdust; placed it in great piles; separated usable pieces of lumber from schwag; and piled up a small mountain of the short pieces. Later in the afternoon, I was supposed to break down the piles of sawdust and short pieces of lumber, move them across the great room, or even outside on the sidewalk. The next morning, I would repeat the "labor." This was my first, and hopefully last union job, the privilege for which I had to cough up more than a few bucks from each weekly paycheck to pay the union bosses. But it was steady work and I needed the money.

With that need satisfied, I yearned to scratch another itch. I had been on a long dry-spell, sexually speaking, and had long given up the quest. Countless rejections had taken their toll on my self-esteem and I found myself making nightly love to a bottle. But one night, as I entered the Suds and Dolls bar in a dreary part of the city, I spotted this thin blonde sitting on a barstool, apparently alone. I don't know why I did it, but I just excused myself and squeezed in between her and the cocktail waitress station. I ordered myself a Bush bottle and then casually looked her way. I had only really wanted to get a better look at a pretty face, expecting nothing more than either being cooly ignored or invited to look elsewhere.

But when I looked over, I was met with a beautiful smile, wide-open blue eyes and a come hither look. I checked the mirror behind the bar because I have too many times fallen for that lowly trick, only to discover the real object of primal affection standing behind me. I must have appeared shocked, as she said in a husky voice, "Well hello there;" but I mustered up the courage to mutter some inane comeback.

And for the first, and probably only time in my miserable life, I left a full bottle of beer on the counter and walked arm in arm with my newfound fantasy. I didn't need to pinch myself to see if this were but a lurid dream; she was doing the pinching and I swelled with pride and lust.

She said she wanted to get high; I told her I had a half-gram of some primo hash back at The Rosemont. She squeezed my inner thigh as I cranked over the engine. At my room, we had only taken a few tokes when she came on like a Penthouse letter, animal-like in her heated desire. We grunted like pigs in heat for a few minutes, then she suggested I spend the night at her house. As we opened the door to leave, a red-faced Ruby blocked our path.

"No girls," she screamed. "Get her out and don't come back."

I was puffed up with testosterone juice and felt invincible. "Screw you, you old hag," I spat. I instantly regretted my outburst, trying to pull back the words; but like a bullet carelessly fired from a gun, they had already penetrated the target.

"You're outta here, mister." Ruby wheezed. "By morning I want all of your things packed and you gone." She wheeled and stomped down the hallway to her shabby apartment, her well-worn blue slippers welling up dust.

After a sleepless night of unbridled lust and a breakfast of steak and eggs, Deanna (we didn't exchange names until the cold light of dawn—this was the early 70s after all) invited me back for an encore. "You bet," I said, leaving for work. But when I got back to The Rosemont, I found out Ruby was a woman of her word. She had three, count 'em, three locks screwed into the outside of my door. I went, hat in hand, to her apartment but she just hissed at me to get the hell out.

"But I need to change clothes and go to work," I whined.

"You should have thought of that when you brought that hussy in here last night."

I was stunned beyond belief: I was locked out and, did I hear her right—hussy?

I spent the better part of the morning hunting down the rightful owner of the flophouse. After a bit of research, I found out that an insurance agent owned the building. I went to his office and told him my story, begging his and Ruby's forgiveness. He was a thin, kindly looking old gent with a pencil-thin mustache and a crisp pin-stripe suit. Both were shiny with use.

After I spilled out my confession of contrition, I waited for his answer. It came like a stab in my heart.

"Well," he said, studying me carefully, seeing only a longhaired, wild hippie sitting before him.

"If you're not good enough to live there, you're just not good enough to live there. Move."

Wait a minute, I thought, not good enough to live in a flophouse full of reeking winos? How far had I slid down the slickpole of life?

At noon I returned to The Rosemont and, under the steely

168

glaze of Ruby, packed up what little belongings I had in my world and carried them out to my van. I met my brother in his room as he was eating a sandwich for lunch. I told him of my misfortune and rhetorically asked what else can go wrong?

"A lot," Jim said, as he tossed me an envelope. "It's your paycheck, they fired you for not showing up this morning."

I drove back to the trailer court that Deanna lived in, but since I have the sense of direction of a beached whale, I could not for the life of me find it. I spent several days on the hunt with no luck. Even the Suds and Dolls workers hadn't seen her.

Later, after spending a week couch surfing, I headed down the open road.

Yellowstone, I noted to myself. I haven't been there in years.

(Bob Beer is a journalist, editor, writer and songwriter living in Telluride, so he doesn't appear to be too out of whack when compared to other residents. He apparently got a bit twisted in the 60s and 70s and carries a few social scars to this day).

Clown Day: A Utah Tradition

by Some Clown

When was the last time you put on a rainbow wig, a big red nose, and shoes five sizes too big? Imagine all of your friends getting so decked out in clown makeup that no one was familiar. You become this anonymous pack of clowns. The tourists laugh and stare. You're putting smiles on their normal faces on top of their normal fashions. You tell them they can join you, but they have to put their clothes on backwards. There are no takers. You don't need drugs…you're the joker, you're the clown shaking everything up and making people laugh.

Funny thing is, not everyone thinks you're so funny. The backdrop of this year's Clown Day at Snowbird was the police presence. Word from the street was police were ready to give 'inciting a riot' tickets to any clowns on the slopes. No tickets were given out, but Clown Day went underground this year. The day went on with celebrations at Solitude and of course, Park City. The mother of all Clowns, Park City, gave her clowns free range.

There's a history behind Clown Day and all of its merrymakers. In the raging 70's, Clown Day started with a parade on Main Street, hit the slopes, and went from there. A victim of its own success, the party hardy attitude got a little too party, and Clown Day was shut down, technically, and most people agreed that it was probably a decision made in the interest of public safety. But Clown Day didn't go away just because they said it should. There's a spirit behind this day that goes beyond the party, the drugs, and the silly outfits. There's something about those silly outfits.

Clown Day was forced underground when Park City's infamous 'clown clause' was born, stating that no clown outfits were to be allowed on the lifts. The party shifted to other resorts. Its band of merry pranksters was clever enough to keep the spirit alive. They snuck clown suits up, under clothes and by chopper drop. They risked repercussion and ridicule, sneaking around like freedom fighters just for the chance to dress and act like a clown.

There is camaraderie amongst these clowns. They come in all shapes, sizes and outfits, but you know a fellow clown when you see one. On the lift ride up, you and all the clowns sing the circus theme—BA da dada bada da da dada, and wonder if they can really arrest you for dressing like a clown. What would the charge be? You shout at each other, "Hey you…you clown," and find out its fun to call your people 'yo clown.' It's the little details that cause the laughter, like the redneck clown with five teeth and braces; the dirt biker with tire tracks all over his riding suit; the midget cowboy riding the ostrich; the neon one-piece ski suits so bright you have to wear sunglasses. Or that guy wearing the horrid red dress and clown make-up who has to be at work in half an hour and he doesn't know how to get his clown make-up off. He might just have to sling food with that smile still on his face. On Clown Day there is never a shortage of laughter.

The time, energy, and creativity put into these outfits is amazing. People start months in advance, with creations like the puppet/puppet master all-in-one outfit, or the hand sequined and beaded clown hat/helmet. Clowns use umbrellas instead of ski poles, or bring up a banana and claim it's their cell phone and shove it in your face saying, "It's for you." Reality is altered, if just for the day. Although if you're one of the clowns, you spend the rest of the year looking and laughing about ideas for next time, giving your imagination a whole new range.

Some clowns wore their season passes from Clown Days of yore and the stack of passes around their necks was two inches thick. The accumulated years of season pass skiing amongst this group is into the hundreds. They've clowned like this for a long time. Many are friends because they met at previous Clown Days.

There were somersaults and jumps. Some clown in a race suit and a hotshot attitude hot-dogged a perfect spread eagle. The clowns cheered everyone on, with this year's cheer reflecting a new attitude, "Go Big, Be Safe." The blow up doll sat watching quietly and obediently until some clown duct taped her to his back and skied off into the sunset.

Advice was exchanged amongst the clowns, "You'd think the elastic would keep the red nose on, but it's hard to ski with this thing. The secret is super glue." You hope that it will come off, but laugh because it may never come off. These days, identifying yourself as a clown isn't the bundle of laughs it used to be. Until next year.

Mormons Don't Want To Be Mormons Anymore

by Clare Goldsberry

Yep, you hear correctly. After 150 years of selling their religion as distinct, separate and exclusive, they now want to be mainstream Christians. Heaven forbid!!

A PR blitz of recent news articles revealed that Mormons are fed up with being... well, Mormons! They want the "M" word to fade into history like polygamy. An article in the Arizona Republic on Sunday, Feb. 18, quoted Dale Bills, a church spokesman in Salt Lake City, saying Mormons "want to be known as followers of and believers in the savior Jesus Christ." He claims mainstream Christianity hasn't understood this.

Now, instead of being referred to as Mormons or "LDS," they want to be called The Church of Jesus Christ—with an emphasis on "Jesus Chris," to prove to the world that they are Christian. So, I guess now instead of calling them Mormons, we'll have to call them "persons of the Church of Jesus Christ." (They still don't want to be referred to as Christians)

It seems that the Mormon Church is facing a huge identity crisis. It's a fitting situation for a group of people whose adherents generally suffer from various degrees of schizophrenia. For over a century, Mormons didn't want to fit into mainstream Protestantism. They insisted on a position that placed them outside the norm, separate in doctrine and dogma, and distinct in religious history as the ONLY TRUE church of Jesus Christ on the planet. It appears that this formula has worked quite as well as Mormons, on paper at least, have outpaced mainstream Protestantism in terms of increasing their membership. Now they want to be like the mainstream Protestants.

To this end, they no longer advertise the Book of Mormon on TV. Instead, viewers are urged to call and get a free copy of the Bible. This switch in advertising tactics happened about the same time that a DNA study out of BYU showed that Native Americans actually did come from peoples of the Northern Asia, probably across the Bering Sea land bridge, as anthropologists have suggested for decades. So much for the "Submarine from Jerusalem" theory! (Quietly, church leaders have been told not to push that story openly anymore)

Another change has been in the Temple ceremonies. The blood oaths have been removed, along with an insulting reference to Protestant ministers as servants of Satan. Church leaders cited the fact that these things were offensive to new converts from mainstream Christianity. Duh! The first time I saw that movie, I knew it wasn't produced by Cecil B. DeMille! If I could have walked out of that theater...!

What's next in their attempt to be seen as "Christians?" Well, I predict that soon they will get rid of their magic underwear. After all, if people see the outline of those "garments," they will for sure know that these people are "Mormons," not Christians.

I also predict that the Mormon Tabernacle Choir (they claim that name will stick) will begin singing music from the "Old Time Gospel Hour." Hymns such as "Give Me That Old Time Religion" and "Old Rugged Cross" ought to be enough to convince all the mainstream Christians that Mormons really aren't weird.

But, I think the thing that will clinch the deal will be the day Church leaders replace the angel Moroni with a gold cross on the SLC Temple spire. That's sure to convince the Christian world that Mormons have finally come into the mainstream, and the "M" word will fade into history, just like polygamy.

I for one, don't think the Mormons should mess with success. Besides, they'll soon become so mainstream that they won't be fun anymore. Utah might become as normal as ... God forbid!... California!

One Phat Tat

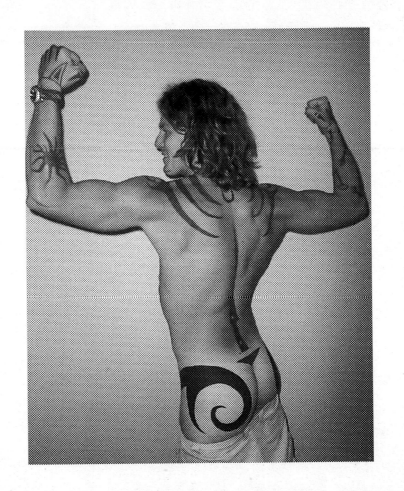

175

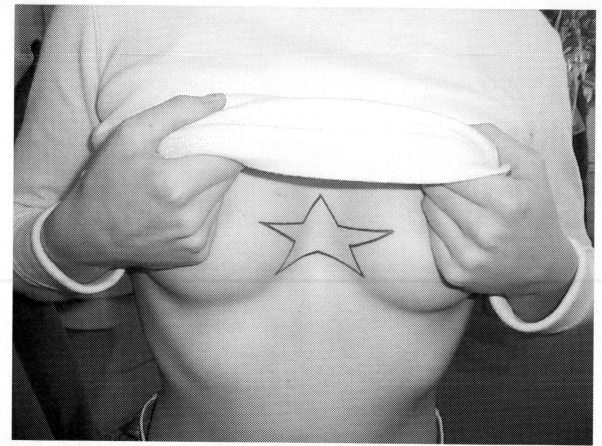

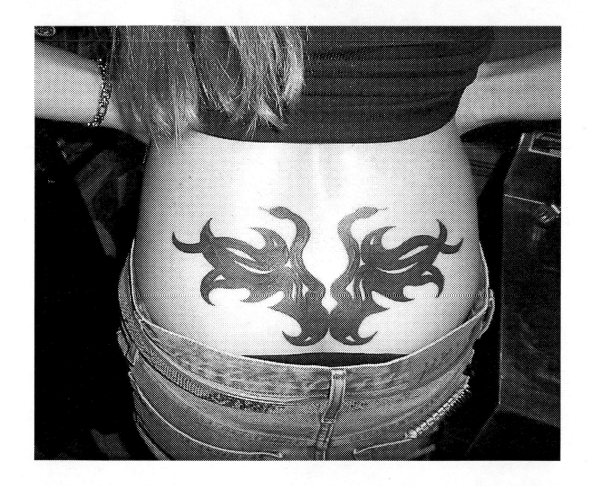

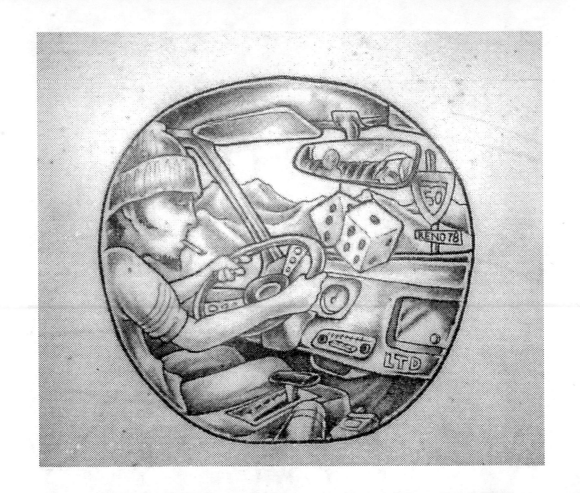

178

179

Recoil In Horror!

(If you can't handle the rough stuff,
Please consider this page the end of the book).

THE END

The Story of Kiki and the Raggot

Though outrageously funny, the story of Kiki and the Raggot is nothing new. Wild Utah has been unable to confirm or dispute the validity of the story, the name of its author, or the accreditation of its first run publication. A simple search engine peek into the word "Raggot" returns countless websites that probably violate a legitimate copyright by running this story. Scores of these websites begin the piece with "This is an actual article from the LA Times..." We contacted the LA Times Syndicate, requesting the reproduction rights to the work for the Wild Utah issue in your hand. Trisha Montecinos replied to us with a short letter stating that the LA Times does not own the rights to the work, does not know who controls them currently, and has no forwarding address for the creator of the work. We, too, are probably violating a copyright by printing this piece. We do so for your benefit. Therefore, in the spirit of Alfred Hitchcock, here is The Story of Kiki and the Raggot.

This is an actual article from the LA Times...

"In retrospect, lighting the match was my big mistake. But I was only trying to retrieve the gerbil," Eric Tomazewski told bemused doctors in the Severe Burn Unit of Salt Lake City Hospital. Tomazewski and his homosexual partner Andrew "Kiki" Farnum had been admitted for emergency treatment after a felching session had gone seriously wrong. "I pushed a cardboard tube up his rectum and slipped Raggot, our gerbil, in," he explained. "As usual, Kiki shouted out 'Armageddon,' my cue that he'd had enough. I tried to retrieve Raggot but he wouldn't come out again, so I peered into the tube and struck a match, thinking the light might attract him."

At a hushed press conference, a hospital spokesman described what happened next. "The match ignited a pocket of intestinal gas and a flame shot out of the tubing, igniting Mr. Tomazewski's hair and severely burning his face. It also set fire to the gerbil's fur and whiskers, which ignited a larger pocket of gas further up the intestine, propelling the rodent out like a cannonball. Tomazewski suffered second-degree burns and a broken nose from the impact of the gerbil, while Farnum suffered first and second degree burns to his anus and lower intestinal tract.

Editor's Notes: Top Ten Scariest Things About This Story
10. "I pushed a cardboard tube up his rectum ...."
9. "So I peered into the tube..." (I'm sorry, but that's like looking through a telescope into hell. I'd rather use binoculars to stare at the sun).
8. That poor gerbil (who obviously suffers from low self-esteem) being shot out of a guy's ass like Rocky the Flying Squirrel on Rocky and Bullwinkle.
7. Suffering a broken nose from a gerbil being launched

out of someone's anus. I'm guessing, but I seriously doubt the gerbil was springtime fresh after his journey in Kiki's "tunnel of love."

6. People walking around with these volcanic-like pockets of gas in their rectums.

5. People who do this kind of thing and then admit what they were doing when taken to the emergency room. Sorry, but I think I would have made up a story about a gang of roving, pyromanical, anal sex fiends breaking into my house and sodomizing me with charcoal lighter fluid before admitting the truth. Call me old fashioned, but I just can't imagine looking at a doctor and saying "Well Doc, it's like this. You see, we have this gerbil named Raggot and we took a cardboard tube..."

4. "First and second degree burns to the anus." Wouldn't this make the burning itch and discomfort of hemorrhoids a welcome relief? How does one ever take a healthy dump after something like this? And the smell of a burning anus must be in the top five most horrible scents on the face of God's green earth.

3. People named "Kiki" which is obviously a Polynesian word for "Idiotic white man who inserts rodents up his butt."

2. What kind of hospital would hold a press conference on this?

1. This happened in Salt Lake City. What kind of people are those Mormons? I am getting a whole new image of the Osmond family.

182

Sexnight at Casa Del Crenshaw

WARNING: This story is truly hideous. It is repulsive, disgusting, and can only be enjoyed by someone with the sickest sense of humor. Enjoy at your own risk.

I have done many regrettable things in my life. But nothing approaches the horrific night crouched in the Pfizer bush outside Mills Crenshaw's bedroom window.

A romantic dinner of Yankee potpie and Jell-O had apparently done the trick for the Crenshaws. The dirty dishes were left for Nyk Fry to do, and off to the bedroom the couple went. Mills retired to the bathroom for a quick coat of Brylcream and to change into his Mr. Mac brown, polyester robe (complete with light brown piping and suede elbow patches).

Mrs. Mills took advantage of the time alone to eat another slice of pie, belch like a fat sailor, and pick her nose. Mills emerged from the bathroom, with purpose. He set the demure mood with the music of John Philip Susa. I sensed an immediate bulge in his robe. His back stiffened, the bulge grew as he gave his less-than-lovely wife a military salute.

Taking the point, Mrs. Mills rose from the bed, her breasts sagging around her waist like a roofer's nail bag. She started what can only be described as a really embarrassing striptease; layer after layer of ZCMI's finest hit the floor until all that was left was this horrid woman, who believe me is only a nosebone and lip plate away from being on the cover of National Geographic. Her panties were both visually pleasing (gray with high tensile steel suspenders), and functional—keeping her

uterus from prolapsing on the expensive carpet like a dead squid. Then off came the last items: panties, hair, teeth, left eye, right leg below the knee. She "assumed the position" on the bed, not unlike a large, desert tortoise flipped over in the sun. She reached beneath the bed and pulled out the Jaws of Life, hooked them up to the hydraulics, and spreads her legs for Millsey.

There it is my friends, deep in the Great Rift Valley, the OLDUVAI GORGE! the land that both time, and personal hygiene products forgot. I can only describe what between her legs looked like as a deflated football stuffed in the mouth of Grizzly Adams...after he had eaten a jam sandwich.

Then it was up to the Red Baron. The robe hit the floor like a flag of surrender. He worked his penis until it has reached its full and glorious length—roughly a cherry stuck on the end of a ballpoint pen. He strode gracefully to his love, carefully tethered himself to the headboard, and proceeded to slap his weenie against the thick fleshy labia, somewhat akin to throwing a hotdog down the hallway.

He was really working, his neck wattle bright crimson and flapping side to side like a 4H, blue-ribbon gobbler. I can describe Mills' "gameface" as looking like he's about to sneeze, then jamming his toe in a light socket. He rose to his knees, let out a scream, and his ejaculate emerged from his glands like the last drop of Visine.

Then it was over. He defecated on the sheets, then sat at the edge of the bed, sobbing into his cupped hands. It was what I can only describe as "very weird." As I looked back, I saw Nyk Fry gathering up the sheets for cleaning, and Mills still sobbing like a child.

183

A Joke For You

A Jew, a Catholic, and a Mormon were having drinks at the bar following an interfaith meeting.

The Jew, bragging on his virility, said, "I have four sons. One more and I'll have a basketball team."

The Catholic poo-pooed this accomplishment, stating, "That's nothing, boy. I have 10 sons, one more and I'll have a football team."

To which the Mormon replied, "You fellas ain't got a clue. I have 17 wives. One more and I'll have a golf course."